C000258559

Dartmoor

Compiled by
Sue Viccars

publishing

Mapping
sourced from   Ordnance Survey

Dedication

For my sons Nick and Joffy, who love Dartmoor too.

Acknowledgements

Special thanks are due to Dr Tom Greeves for kindly casting his expert eye over my manuscript, and for fine-tuning historical details. I'd also like to thank Sarah Letts at Jarrold for giving me the perfect excuse for spending the summer months exploring Dartmoor in detail, and all those friends who willingly kept me company while I was 'working' – and especially Brenda, both for her help with photography and for her patient support.

Text:	Sue Viccars
Photography:	Sue Viccars
Editorial:	Ark Creative, Norwich
Design:	Ark Creative, Norwich

© Jarrold Publishing 2005

 Ordnance Survey® This product includes mapping data licensed from Ordnance Survey® with the permission of the Controller of Her Majesty's Stationery Office. © Crown Copyright 2005. All rights reserved. Licence number 100017593. Ordnance Survey, the OS symbol and Pathfinder are registered trademarks and Explorer, Landranger and Outdoor Leisure are trademarks of the Ordnance Survey, the national mapping agency of Great Britain.

ISBN 0-7117-2089-4

While every care has been taken to ensure the accuracy of the route directions, the publishers cannot accept responsibility for errors or omissions, or for changes in details given. The countryside is not static: hedges and fences can be removed, field boundaries can alter, footpaths can be rerouted and changes in ownership can result in the closure or diversion of some concessionary paths. Also, paths that are easy and pleasant for walking in fine conditions may become slippery, muddy and difficult in wet weather, while stepping stones across rivers and streams may become impassable.

If you find an inaccuracy in either the text or maps, please write to or e-mail Jarrold Publishing at one of the addresses below.

First published 2002
by Jarrold Publishing
Revised and reprinted 2005.

Printed in Singapore. 3/05
by Craft Print International Limited

Jarrold Publishing
Pathfinder Guides, Whitefriars,
Norwich NR3 1JR
email: info@totalwalking.co.uk
www.totalwalking.co.uk

Front cover: Birch Tor
Previous page: River Plym below Cadover Bridge

Contents

Keymap

SCALE 1:277 777 or 1 INCH to about 4½ MILES 1CM to 2.7KM

0   2   4   6   8   10 KILOMETRES   15

0   2   4   6 MILES 8   10

KEYMAP HEIGHTS SHOWN IN FEET

Introduction

Dartmoor, the largest area of wild country in southern Britain, is somewhere that gets under the skin. Those who move to the area from elsewhere in the country either love it or loathe it; those born there may go away for a while, but tend to gravitate back sooner or later. Thousands of people simply miss Dartmoor altogether as they race through Devon each summer on the main roads around the north and south of the moor en route for a Cornish holiday. But from both the A38 in the south, and the A30 that skirts the northern edge of Dartmoor, you can get a tantalising glimpse of what lies beyond these tourist routes in the form of great swells of open moorland beyond South Brent and south of Okehampton. The eastern approach to the moor, along the B3212 via the undulating hills and wooded river valleys west of Exeter, is quite different, and brings with it a wonderful sense of anticipation as the moorland landscape unfolds beyond Moretonhampstead.

A varied landscape

Dartmoor is part of a vast, raised granite plateau, rising to 2,037ft (621m) at its highest point, High Willhays, that stretches for many miles to the west, emerging again at Bodmin Moor in Cornwall, and the Isles of Scilly, lying 28 miles (45km) west-south-west of Land's End. The moor receives the full force of the prevailing south-westerly winds, and has an annual rainfall often more than 60in (150cm). It can be a bleak and forbidding place in bad weather. Where the granite has been exposed to the elements frost, wind and rain have weathered it into fantastic blocks and shapes to form 'tors', the most famous and accessible of which is Haytor on the southern side of the moor. Further erosion of the granite blocks has resulted in clitter, small granite boulders, covering large areas on the slopes beneath the tors.

The Rugglestone Inn, Widecombe

Blackator Copse

But Dartmoor is so much more than a wild moorland. The high annual rainfall and unyielding granite has given rise to a number of beautiful rivers, most of which have their sources on the northern moor. Millions of years ago the granite plateau was tilted, so that the highest land now lies on the north and west of the moor, and most of the rivers flow south, emerging from areas of inhospitable bog to form small, sparkling moorland streams. Where they hit the softer shales, slates and limestone at the granite edge they have cut deep valleys, now thickly wooded – the Teign gorge at Castle Drogo, the Dart below Dr Blackall's Drive, the Avon and the Erme – which provide wonderful walking opportunities.

The human imprint

At first sight it is easy to believe that Dartmoor is a totally natural landscape, but nothing could be farther from the truth. The moor has been settled since prehistoric times, and the wealth of Bronze Age remains, in the form of standing stones, stone circles and rows, enclosures and hut circles, is unrivalled elsewhere in the country. Dating from 2500BC to 750BC, about 5,000 hut circles have been identified, and it has been estimated that there could have been several thousand people living on the moor at that time in settlements such as that at Grimspound.

Iron Age occupation is evident in the form of hillforts and earthworks, such as those near the Dewerstone, and at Prestonbury Camp and Cranbrook Castle, overlooking the Teign gorge.

There has been plenty of industry, too: the moor has been mined for tin since medieval times, and evidence today is plentiful in the form of gullies and pits, and the ruins of huts and blowing houses, where tin was smelted. A system of leats (narrow channels carrying water) was created to improve water supplies to farms, mills and tin works, and latterly to supply the growing population of Plymouth. Many of these provide excellent routes for walkers today, as do the abandoned trackways associated with the disused granite quarries to be found near Princetown and Haytor. In more recent times, a number of reservoirs have been built around the fringes of the open moor, and these again offer great walking opportunities for those looking for a gentler route.

Dartmoor today

Dartmoor was given National Park status in 1951, and is managed by the Dartmoor National Park Authority. Operating from their headquarters at Parke in Bovey Tracey, the authority has the task of balancing the conflicting demands made on Dartmoor: those of agriculture, tourism,

Crazywell Pool

Ruins near Foggintor Quarry

conservation, and the controversial use of part of the moor as a training ground for the army. Walkers should be aware of what purposes lie behind the creation of the National Parks: '...the conservation of the natural beauty, wildlife and cultural heritage of the area, and the promotion of the understanding and enjoyment of its special qualities by the public'.

In accordance with the wishes of the park authority, there is no doubt that the best way to explore Dartmoor is on foot. The walks in this book have all been devised to introduce the walker to a wide range of experiences, ranging from a gentle stroll through the forests around a moorland reservoir, to a tougher route across the open moor to explore the upper reaches of one of Dartmoor's loveliest rivers. The routes suggested avoid the 'honeypot' areas and concentrate instead on getting as far off the beaten track as possible, as quickly as possible, yet without tackling those vast, almost featureless expanses of high moorland where competent navigational skills are essential. As with any area of high ground, weather conditions can change rapidly, and the moor can be fog-bound even in mid-summer; for this reason only Walks 2, 7 and 8 are suitable in all weathers.

Brick Cottage, Leusdon

1 Birch Tor and Vitifer Mines

START On the B3212 east of the Warren House Inn

DISTANCE 1¾ miles (2.8km)

TIME 1 hour

PARKING Bennett's Cross car park (free)

ROUTE FEATURES Narrow moorland path to Birch Tor; short clamber out of heathery gully towards end of walk

This easy yet fascinating walk skirts around the edge of one of the most significant areas of heather moorland on Dartmoor, much of it classified as an SSSI (Site of Special Scientific Interest). It is prized not only for its wealth of rare lichens and birds, but also for the extensive and accessible evidence of the area's industrial heritage in the form of tin-mining gullies and workings.

Bennett's Cross

Before you set out on this walk take a look at Bennett's Cross, just above the car park. This simple granite cross is named after a 16th-century miner. It is also on the line of the ancient track across the moor, followed today by the modern road, which dates from the

Tin has been mined on Dartmoor since medieval times. **Vitifer, Birch Tor** and **Golden Dagger mines** were among the most important on Dartmoor, being worked extensively in the 19th and early 20th centuries. The last mine closed in 1930.

PUBLIC TRANSPORT Bus service from Exeter (via Moretonhampstead) and Plymouth

REFRESHMENTS Warren House Inn just south west of the car park

PUBLIC TOILETS None en route; at the Warren House Inn when open

ORDNANCE SURVEY MAPS Explorer OL28 (Dartmoor), Landranger 191 (Okehampton & North Dartmoor)

late 18th century. Once at the cross, turn away from the road and walk towards the moor to meet a clear path (Two Moors Way) at right angles.

Ⓐ Turn left and follow the path uphill. At the crest of the hill turn right by a modern cairn (pile of stones) and take the narrow path through the heather to gain the top of Birch Tor, from which there are wonderful views of Grimspound and Hamel Down across the Challacombe valley to the left, and over the mine workings at Vitifer to the right. Walk straight ahead from the tor and downhill on a narrow

Grimspound, thought by many to be Dartmoor's finest prehistoric site, dates from around 1300BC. Situated below Hameldown Tor beside the Grimslake stream, it must have provided an attractive site, with good grazing, and was probably used for keeping stock safe. The remains of about two dozen hut circles have been found within the enclosure wall. The site's significance was fully realised through investigations by the Dartmoor Exploration Committee in 1894.

well-worn path to meet a deep-cut stony path at a T-junction. (If you want to visit Grimspound, turn left here to pass Headland Warren farm and gain the road, then turn right.)

? *In what year was the fire – that has never been allowed to go out – in the Warren House Inn first established?*

B Turn right and pick your way along the rocky path, which becomes grassier as it drops down into the valley. This area is lovely all year round, with white hawthorn blossom in May and young bracken in June, gorse and heather in late summer, and bright red rowan berries in the autumn. At the valley bottom the path reaches a grassy track that runs along the valley from the Golden Dagger tin mine.

Turn right and walk along the valley to reach a junction of paths **C**. The path left crosses the stream: it is a great picnic spot, with various granite ruins and enclosures. *Be aware, however, that some of the gullies and pits may be deep; keep an eye on your children.* If you want to go to the Warren House Inn at this point, turn left over the stream, then straight up the hill on an obvious track; this popular pub soon comes into view. It is said to be the third-highest pub in England, at 1,400ft (427m) above sea level.

To return to your car, go straight on, keeping the stream on the left. A few minutes later the path forks; take the right path, and walk uphill along a narrow, gritty path that crosses another small stream and passes an area of snaking willows on the right, then under a pretty rowan tree. The path levels off to enter a deep, flat-bottomed, grassy gully. Keep going to the end of the gully where you have to scramble up and out of it to the left; then veer right through the heather to reach a narrow path at right angles. Turn right to return to the Bennett's Cross car park. **●**

Birch Tor

Chagford and the River Teign

START Chagford

DISTANCE 2 miles (3.2km)

TIME 1 hour

PARKING Non-paying car park past the church

ROUTE FEATURES No difficulties

2

Chagford is one of Dartmoor's most appealing small town, a popular tourist destination nestling beneath lofty Meldon and Nattadon Commons on the north-eastern edge of the moor. With a fascinating history and a wealth of attractive buildings, it provides the perfect base for an easy walk through narrow, flower-filled streets to the lovely meadows along the River Teign, and back via the old market square and church.

Chagford was confirmed by Edward I in 1305 as a stannary town where tin metal was brought for assaying and taxation, the whole process being known as the 'coinage' of tin. The other stannary towns were Tavistock, Ashburton and Plympton. At one time 40 per cent of Devon's tin production passed through Chagford, and it remained an important stannary town until the mid-17th century.

Leave the car park and turn left down the lane. Turn right down the High Street, past the

Three Crowns Hotel on the left, said to be haunted by the ghost of Royalist Sidney Godolphin, who died of musket wounds here in 1643 during the Civil War.

A Chagford was for many years an important market town. On reaching the square note the

? In the church there are a number of carved roof bosses. One shows three linked animals – can you see what they are?

PUBLIC TRANSPORT Bus service from Exeter and Okehampton

REFRESHMENTS The Three Crowns Hotel, the Globe, the Buller's Arms and the Ring of Bells; also several cafés in Chagford

PUBLIC TOILETS In the Pepper Pot in the square

PICNIC/PLAY AREA In Jubilee Park, by the car park

ORDNANCE SURVEY MAPS Explorer OL28 (Dartmoor), Landranger 191 (Okehampton & North Dartmoor)

'Pepper Pot', an octagonal market house, built in 1862 by Rev George Hayter Hames. Hames sponsored various town improvements, including a proper drainage system and water supply, and the installation of gas. In 1891 Chagford also became one of the first towns to enjoy water-powered electric street lighting. Continue straight on down Mill Street; at the fork keep right (Mill Street) downhill, signed Gidleigh and

The **church of St Michael the Archangel** dates from the 15th century, but was much restored in the 19th century. Look for the inscription to Mary Whiddon on the sanctuary floor. The story goes that she was shot on the church steps immediately after her wedding on October 11, 1641; some say that R.D. Blackmore based part of his novel *Lorna Doone* on this tale.

Throwleigh. At the bottom of the hill the lane veers right (Gidleigh Park Hotel straight on). The lane leads over one bridge, then crosses Chagford Bridge over the River Teign. There has been a bridge here since at least 1224, at the site of the ford that gave Chagford its name: 'chag' is dialect for gorse, hence 'Chagford'.

B Once over the bridge, turn right through a wooden gate on the Two Moors Way (no footpath sign). The path soon passes through a small wooden gate before leading right, over a broken-down granite wall, to run along the river's edge. Note the huge oak trees to the left, growing out of the remains of the old granite wall. Pass through a wooden gate at the field end, and continue to reach an open area, with bracken where paddling is possible. An old mill lies on the opposite bank; with the demise of the tin industry, around 1700, Chagford played a significant role in the woollen industry, spinning wool for the prosperous weaving towns of East Devon. Later, around the mid-19th century, the town developed as a moorland holiday resort.

C Pass through a small, wooden gate and along the bottom of a large field, then over a wooden footbridge/gate, then another footbridge/gate, to enter mixed woodland by the weir. The path leaves the river to follow a leat (trench) on the right. Leave the woodland over a stile/gate, walk along the bottom of the next field, and through a wooden gate. At the end of the next field pass through a small wooden gate at a junction of paths; go straight on (signed Rushford Bridge). Walk through a strip of woodland, over a railed footbridge to enter a field, then diagonally left through a gap in the hedge. Follow the path sign across the next field to join the lane via a gate.

D Turn right to cross Rushford Bridge; walk up the lane to meet the road. Turn right to pass the garage (left) and primary school (right). As you approach the square fork left at the bank, then under the archway into the churchyard. Keeping the church on the left, walk around the west end to find the south door. On leaving the church go straight ahead to meet the lane to the car park. ●

From Chagford churchyard

3 *Haytor Quarry and Tramway*

A gentle stroll across open moorland from the popular car park at Haytor leads to all kinds of surprises (and provides the opportunity to avoid the crowds ascending the slopes to Haytor Rocks). The route

START On the B3387 near Haytor

DISTANCE 1½ miles (2.4km)

TIME 1 hour

PARKING In the lower Haytor car park (with National Park information centre)

ROUTE FEATURES No difficulties

leads to the old Haytor Quarry before returning along the granite tramway, hinting that, historically, there is more to this part of the moor than meets the eye.

From the car park cross the road and walk straight ahead between two granite boulders on a broad, grassy path, running slightly uphill. Aim for the right side of the quarry spoil heaps that soon come into view ahead, and proceed to join a flat, grassy area to their right.

Ⓐ Cross the flat area, and veer left; ahead you will see a deeply banked gully that leads into the quarry. Walk up the bank to the left of the gully, and then turn right through a small wooden gate in the wire fence. Once through the gate,

follow the narrow path towards the first of two deep ponds. This is

Haytor Rocks are the most popular, accessible and easily recognised of Dartmoor's tors. Those who would never dare to venture farther into the heart of the moor are happy to take the short walk up to the base of these spectacular rocks, rising 1,499ft (457m) above sea level. Their appeal as a tourist attraction first became apparent during the Victorian period. Fortunately, an early 20th-century scheme to construct a coal-fired electric tramway to improve access to the rocks came to naught.

PUBLIC TRANSPORT Bus service from Exeter, Newton Abbot, Tavistock, Totnes

REFRESHMENTS Ice cream van in car park; the Rock Inn at Haytor Vale just to the east

PUBLIC TOILETS In car park

ORDNANCE SURVEY MAPS Explorer OL28 (Dartmoor), Landranger 191 (Okehampton & North Dartmoor)

a great picnic spot, and wonderfully tranquil. Look around carefully and you will find all sorts of bolts and rings in the rocks, and some iron winding gear still visible in the water: a reminder of the time around 100 men worked here. Quarrying began in 1820 under the ownership of George Templer (1781–1843) of Stover, when granite from Haytor was reputedly the cheapest on Dartmoor. The quarry was expanded in 1825 when it won the contract for supplying granite for work at

The Rock Inn sign

the British Museum and for the arches of London Bridge. It fell largely into disuse around 1865 in the face of cheaper competition from Cornwall.

B Walk around the left bank of the two pools – look out for goldfish – to leave the quarry via a narrow, sandy path at the far end of second pool. This emerges through a bank to join a grassy path; walk straight ahead to meet the granite railway at right angles.

Tranquil waters in Haytor Quarry

George Templer built the railway to transport granite eight miles (12.9km) to the head of the Stover Canal (built by his father, James, in 1792) at Teigngrace, from where it would be conveyed by barge to Teignmouth. By 1858 the railway was disused.

C Turn right and follow the granite railway across the open moor, with stunning views to the left towards Greator Rocks and Hound Tor over the valley of the Becka Brook. The railway curves right to reach a junction; follow the 'branchline' over a small embankment towards the quarry, to reach the level area just below the spoil heap. Various bumps and gullies to the side of the railway here indicate the site of a small community, where Templer built cottages, a pub and possibly a school for his workers. Later, in 1825, more cottages were built in Haytor Vale; the Rock Inn was originally the single-workers' hostel.

D From the end of the quarry turn left to retrace your steps down the grassy path to the car park. ●

The **granite railway**, the first of its kind in Devon, was opened on September 16, 1820. Its design is simple; cheap, readily available granite was used to form flanged rails, along which teams of up to 18 horses pulled wooden-wheeled, open-sided, flat-bed carts. Fortunately, most of its route to the head of the Stover Canal runs slightly downhill.

? *How many sets of points can you find on this section of the granite tramway?*

Hound Tor and Hayne Down

For views of the greatest number of tors in a small area, this has to be one of the best short walks on Dartmoor. It is also packed with all kinds of legends and stories, and ends at the ruined medieval village on Houndtor Down, best seen on a sunny day in May when the slopes are covered with a shimmering azure carpet of bluebells.

START Hound Tor

DISTANCE 3¼ miles (5.2km)

TIME 2 hours

PARKING Hound Tor car park (free) at Swallerton Gate

ROUTE FEATURES Uneven rocky path from Hayne Down to Hayne; steep climb up the lane from Great Houndtor Farm to the cattle-grid

4

🖉 Leave the car park and turn right. Hound Tor 1,358ft (414m), said to resemble a pack of hounds frozen in flight, rises craggily before you. At Swallerton Gate turn right and walk past the thatched Dartmoor longhouse on the left, originally a pub. Ignore the small lane running off to the right (unsuitable for motor vehicles), and walk along the grassy bank on

Near Hound Tor

the right of the lane. Look left for views of Honeybag and Chinkwell Tors, and the swell of Hamel Down beyond. Jay's Grave is soon reached at the edge of beechwoods on the left; the pointed hill ahead in the distance is Easdon Tor.

Ⓐ Turn right on the bridlepath through a small wooden gate and

PUBLIC TRANSPORT None available

REFRESHMENTS Mobile refreshments van in car park during holiday periods and weekends – 'The Hound of the Basket Meals'

PUBLIC TOILETS None en route

ORDNANCE SURVEY MAPS Explorer OL28 (Dartmoor), Landranger 191 (Okehampton & North Dartmoor)

up the grassy slope, with the wire fence left. At the top of the hill amazing views of Dartmoor's tors open up. Note Haytor Rocks to the south, and the quarry at Holwell Tor; you can also pick out the line of the granite tramway along Haytor Down. Pass through a small wooden gate, then an old granite wall, and straight on, keeping the fence on the left. Views of Hayne Down open up ahead; look

Bowerman's Nose, towering nearly 40ft (12.25m) high, is a natural feature – but local legend tells the story of an 11th-century hunter, Bowerman, who disturbed a coven of witches. In revenge, they encased him in stone, and although his family searched high and low they found no trace of him. There he stands to this day, regretting the folly of his ways.

towards the left slope of the down to see the distinctive outline of Bowerman's Nose. Walk downhill, through a small wooden gate, then down the field, keeping a large gorse bush left, and aiming for the bottom left corner. Leave the field via a small wooden gate to reach the lane.

B Turn left through Moyles Gate. Turn right up a grassy path (slightly boggy in winter); ignore a path that leads left towards Bowerman's Nose. There are two rocky outcrops on top of the hill ahead; aim for the right side of the left outcrop. The path becomes narrow and rocky, and passes over the grassy saddle between the two outcrops. Drop down the other side of Hayne Down, through the bracken, with great views towards Manaton Church and Hunter's Tor beyond the Bovey valley. The path reaches a granite wall (left), and ends at a gate. Go through the gate and downhill through a wooded area to pass Hayne on the left, then down a gritty drive to reach Hayne Cross.

C Turn right along the quiet lane to pass Southcott Farm. The lane undulates before dropping down to pass Great Houndtor Farm on the

Jay's Grave

right, and then climbs very steeply up to the cattle-grid at the edge of Houndtor Down.

D Turn left along the narrow bridlepath (Black Hill and Haytor Down). Where the path splits and the bridlepath is signed right, keep left to reach the ruined medieval village, with Greator Rocks beyond – a great picnic spot. Originally the site of a Bronze Age settlement, the village may have been reoccupied around the 9th century, but constructed of wood and turf. Walk up the broad grassy path to the left of the one on which you arrived, making directly for Hound Tor, to pass to the left of the main outcrop, then straight downhill to the car park. ●

> **Kitty Jay** was the daughter of a tenant farmer, who was betrayed by the son of a local landowner. When he refused to marry her she hanged herself, and was buried without ceremony at the cross-roads on Hayne Down. Years later, her bones were excavated and reburied in the simple grave that can be seen today. You will always find flowers here, sometimes said to be the work of a ghostly hand who refuses to let Kitty's sad story be forgotten.

> **?** *Where will you find Winnie the Pooh and Piglet on this walk?*

5 *Lydford*

START Lydford
DISTANCE 2¼ miles (3.6km)
TIME 1 hour
PARKING Car park (free) in the village
ROUTE FEATURES No difficulties

The pretty village of Lydford, nestling on the western edge of the moor, is a somewhat misleading place: in medieval times its prison, court and fearsome reputation for justice were legendary. This gentle walk touches on every aspect of the village's long and fascinating history, as well as taking in two pubs and skirting the edge of the open moor.

Leave the car park and turn right. Just past the Nicholls Hall on the left, turn right along Silver Street, so named because Lydford was home to one of Devon's four mints in the time of Aethelred II (AD979–1026), producing silver pennies. Examples of these can be seen in the 16th-century Castle Inn, opposite the car park. Where the tarmac lane ends (private drive left) keep right and follow the gritty, sometimes muddy track downhill to reach a junction of paths.

Just west of the village lies **Lydford Gorge**, cared for by the National Trust, and well worth a visit. The River Lyd has cut through the 1½ mile- (2.4km-) long gorge via a series of crashing waterfalls and whirlpools – the most impressive being the spectacular 30m (98ft) White Lady waterfall and the Devil's Cauldron – which can be seen from several lovely woodland walks. There is also a shop and café on the site.

Ⓐ A tarmac lane comes in from the left; the Lych Way is signed right. St Petrock's Church used to

PUBLIC TRANSPORT Bus services from Barnstaple, Exeter, Okehampton, Plymouth, Tavistock
REFRESHMENTS The Castle Inn and Hotel, Lydford; Dartmoor Inn at the Lydford turning on the A386
PUBLIC TOILETS In the car park
ORDNANCE SURVEY MAPS Explorer OL28 (Dartmoor), Landranger 191 (Okehampton & North Dartmoor)

be the parish church for much of Dartmoor, and before AD1260 the dead were carried here for burial from as far away as the Postbridge district. The route became known as the Lych Way (*lich* meaning corpse). Walk straight ahead, slightly uphill, to pass beneath the railway bridge (part of the Lydford Junction–Okehampton line, which operated from 1874–1968). At the next fork, keep right to pass between high hedges; the narrow path dips down to pass Kitts Cottage on the right, then runs up to meet the A386.

Lydford Castle

B Cross the road with care, and walk up the bridlepath opposite, which ends at a five-bar gate between granite gateposts. Walk through the gate to pass Highdown on the right, and onto open grassy moorland, with wonderful views of Doe Tor 1,394ft (425m) to the right. The Doetor Brook valley, between Doe Tor and Brat Tor, is home to a wealth of tin-mining remains, based around the Wheal Frederick mine. Notice too, Brat Tor 1,483ft (452m) with a spectacular 13ft-(4m-) high cross

A 'burh', or defended settlement, was created here in Saxon times, as part of a network to protect southern England from Viking raids. There are actually two castles at **Lydford**: a small Norman ringwork dating from around 1087, and the impressive freestanding tower, built in the late 12th century as a prison and courtroom. Lydford became the administrative centre for the old Forest of Dartmoor, and had jurisdiction over the stannary districts of Devon. The prison was used by the Royalists during the Civil War, and was abandoned by the late 17th century.

What is the inscription on the casing of the old drinking fountain which can be found near the driveway to Castle Lea and St Petrock's?

on its summit. Instigated by the well-known Dartmoor artist F.J.Widgery, this commemorates Queen Victoria's Golden Jubilee in 1887. Follow the wall and line of beech trees on the left to pass along the edge of High Down; look out for views of Lydford village and castle to the left. The wall curves left; pass through a gate with a parking area on the right. Follow the gritty track downhill and through another gate; walk on to reach the A386, just to the right of the Dartmoor Inn.

C Cross the road (garage and post office to the right),

and follow the lane opposite back into Lydford village, passing the Granite Way (cycle path) and the war memorial (at Rowell Cross) on the way. To take a look at St Petrock's Church, walk past the car park entrance and past the medieval 'castle'. The original Saxon church was probably constructed of wood; the first reference to a stone building dates to 1237, with restoration in the 15th and early 20th centuries. Dedicated to the Celtic saint St Petrock, who arrived in Cornwall in the 6th century, the church is famous for its superb woodcarvings and beautifully engraved tombstones, including that of George Routledge, a watchmaker who died in 1802: 'Wound up… In hopes of being taken in hand… By his Maker… And of being thoroughly cleaned, repaired… And set-going… In the world to come'. ●

Lydford church

North and South Brentor

6

This walk provides a chance to explore the quiet westernmost corner of the Dartmoor National Park. The prominent landmark of Brent Tor church, perched on a rocky outcrop 1,000ft (335m) above sea level, is instantly recognisable for many miles around and is a fascinating place, both in terms of its geology and its legendary links with the Devil.

START Gibbet Hill
DISTANCE 3 miles (4.8km) with possible 1½ mile (2.4km) extension
TIME 1½ hours (plus 1 hour)
PARKING In a lay-by on the left just over the cattle-grid on the moorland lane between Mary Tavy and North Brentor
ROUTE FEATURES Rocky uneven descent to Wortha Mill

Cross over the lane from your car to pick up a grassy path running left around the contours of Gibbet Hill. Follow this indistinct path downhill to join the tarmac lane opposite two big granite gateposts in the beech-lined wall opposite (the entrance to Wortha).

A Turn right along the lane, which veers left and drops down to reach a cattle-grid and wooden gate. Go through the gate and

Brent Tor church

PUBLIC TRANSPORT Bus service from Okehampton and Tavistock (to Brent Tor) summer only; from Plymouth and Barnstaple (to North Brentor only) all year
REFRESHMENTS None en route; the Brentor Inn on the road between Brent Tor church and the turning to North Brentor; the Castle Inn at Lydford 2½ miles (4km) to the north
PUBLIC TOILETS None en route; in car park for Brent Tor church (plus information board)
PICNIC/PLAY AREA In North Brentor, signed right from the war memorial
ORDNANCE SURVEY MAPS Explorer 112 (Launceston & Holsworthy), Landranger 191 (Okehampton & North Dartmoor)

down the lane to pass the old railway station on the left. The lane crosses the disused railway line, veers left and then right uphill to pass North Brentor village hall (right) and Christ church (right). North Brentor was added to the parish of Brent Tor in 1880, after which date all burials took place in the village; it was very difficult to dig a deep enough grave on the top of Brent Tor. Walk on to reach the T-junction by the 1914–18 war memorial, with bus shelter opposite.

B Turn left. After a few yards the lane bends right. Turn left along a narrow lane to pass pretty cottages; the lane leads into a green lane signed 'South Brentor'. The green lane forks; keep left, and, where the lane sweeps to the right of a gate, follow the small footpath sign through the gate. Walk straight on, keeping the wall right, to pass through an open gateway at the end of the field. Go straight across the next field, and through a small kissing-gate in the next hedge. Keep straight ahead and downhill to pass through another small kissing-gate, just by a ruined building (left). The next footpath sign

> **North Brentor** lies on the route of the old Southern Railway line from Tavistock to Lydford Junction. The station was opened on June 2, 1890, and is now in private ownership – but from the lane you can still see the post box, the Victorian platform canopy, and the sign for the gents' toilets.

points diagonally up the next field towards the top right corner. Leave the field over a small stile, and walk straight on, passing to the left of a gorsy embanked area (enclosing a muddy pond) to leave the field via a gate and stile in the top right corner. Walk down the green lane, with great views of Brent Tor to the right, to meet another green lane at a T-junction near South Brentor Farm.

Village hall, North Brentor

C Turn left and follow the green lane steeply and rockily downhill between high banks. This section can be muddy in winter. The path crosses the River Burn and the old railway line via twin bridges – Wortha Mill Bridge – then runs

uphill to pass the ruins of Wortha Mill, an old corn-grinding mill, on the left. The track becomes tarmac at the entrance to Blacknor Park (right), then leads over a cattle-grid to join the lane on the edge of Gibbet Hill. Turn right and walk along the lane to your car.

Note: If you want to visit Brent Tor church turn right at **C** *and follow the lane until it bends sharp left; turn right (unmarked path) through an old wooden gate and walk through the field, keeping the hedge on the left, to meet the road. Turn right for the church, car park and toilets.* ●

Brent Tor is not formed of granite; it is a remnant of the mass of lava that poured out onto the seabed here more than 300 million years ago. The church of St Michael de Rupe was built around 1130, with alterations in the 13th and 15th centuries, and is the fourth smallest complete parish church in England. Rumour has it that while the church was being built the Devil, displeased with what was going on, hurled stones from the top of the tor onto the unfortunate parishioners below – but he lost the battle.

? *Somewhere near the church you will see a little spring bubbling out of a pipe, which used to supply the village with water. What is its date?*

7 The Teign Gorge at Castle Drogo

START Between Sandy Park and Castle Drogo
DISTANCE 2½ miles (4km)
TIME 1¼ hours
PARKING At the side of the lane opposite the entrance to Coombe Farm and Gibhouse
ROUTE FEATURES No difficulties; dogs are not allowed into Castle Drogo and gardens

A gentle stroll along level paths high above the stunningly beautiful wooded River Teign gorge, with glorious views over Dartmoor. The walk leads below Castle Drogo, one of architect Sir Edwin Lutyens' finest works, set in a commanding position and famous as the 'youngest' castle in the country. The castle and estate have been under the care of the National Trust since 1974.

Castle Drogo's main entrance

 Cross over the lane (which is very quiet) and turn right through a small gate next to a cattle-grid. Follow the concrete lane (signposted Hunter's and Fisherman's Paths) to the end of the field.

A Where the lane becomes tarmac, turn left to leave it and pass through a small wooden gate under beech trees (signposted Hunter's Path). At this point you join a stretch of the Two Moors Way. *(Note: If you feel like a longer*

PUBLIC TRANSPORT Bus service from Okehampton, Newton Abbot and Exeter
REFRESHMENTS National Trust shop and café at the castle; also picnic area; Drewe Arms in Drewsteignton; Sandy Park Inn at Sandy Park
PUBLIC TOILETS By the café and shop
PICNIC/PLAY AREA By the picnic area
ORDNANCE SURVEY MAPS Explorer OL28 (Dartmoor), Landranger 191 (Okehampton & North Dartmoor)

walk, you can go straight ahead here along the lane to reach the river, and then follow signs for the Fisherman's Path along the river to Fingle Bridge, and then take the Hunter's Path all the way back to the castle.) At this point the walk enters the Castle Drogo estate. Follow the broad, level, flinty path along the valley side, with wonderful views opening up to the right, and Castle Drogo towering above you at the top of the

> The **Teign gorge** was the site of significant activity long before Julius Drewe set about realising his dream. On the precipitously steep slopes above Fingle Bridge, a little farther down the gorge, lie Prestonbury Castle Iron Age hillfort, with its twin, Cranbrook Castle, on the hilltop opposite, built by Celtic peoples around 750BC–AD50.

bracken-covered slope on the left. The path bends sharply left at Hunter's Tor to run above the Teign gorge; look ahead to see the craggy outcrop of Sharp Tor. Continue along the path, which falls very steeply away to the right; listen to the sounds of the river below as it rushes over rocks and boulders.

B Ignore a small flight of wooden steps on the left that lead up to the castle, and continue on to pass Sharp Tor; it is worth walking out onto the top of the outcrop, *but take great care.*

C Where a small path and steps appear left, turn left uphill, then almost immediately left again (signed Castle Drogo and Piddledown Common). Keep straight on, with views of the castle opening up ahead, to pass along the Gorse Blossom walk. Ignoring all minor offshoots, keep on the main path which meets the main drive to the castle. Turn left along the drive, and then right to gain the entrance to the car park, café and shop. Note the big granite block at the café entrance, which comes from Blackenstone Quarry, responsible for supplying granite for the building works between 1910 and 1930.

Hunter's Path

> **?** *How was granite for building Castle Drogo transported to the castle?*

Castle Drogo is one of Dartmoor's gems. Spectacularly situated high above the gorge of the Teign river, 1,000ft (305m) above sea level, it resulted from a successful collaboration between Sir Edwin

Lutyens (1869–1944) and self-made millionaire Julius Drewe, who decided to establish his family seat here because he believed that his ancestors had connections with the nearby village of Drewsteignton.

D To return to your car, retrace your steps out of the car park and turn left along the drive; almost immediately (and before you reach the end of the Gorse Blossom walk) turn right (signed Hunter's Path) down a narrow path. At the next footpath sign keep straight on downhill, then down two flights of wooden steps, to reach the Hunter's Path.

Turn right and follow the path all the way back to your car, enjoying superb views towards Dartmoor. ●

It's well worth taking some time to explore both the **Drogo Castle**, which certainly fulfils Lutyens' ambition of combining the qualities and grandeur of a medieval castle with those of a comfortable 20th-century home (part of which is still inhabited) and the beautiful terraced formal gardens, designed in 1915. There is also a delightful woodland spring garden, with rhododendrons, azaleas and camellias, and an impressive circular yew-hedged croquet lawn.

Trenchford and Tottiford Reservoirs

START Trenchford Reservoir
DISTANCE 2½ miles (4km)
TIME 1¼ hours
PARKING In the car park for Trenchford reservoir (contributions cairn) at Bullaton Cross
ROUTE FEATURES No difficulties

This is a peaceful walk through quiet forests and around tranquil reservoirs – especially lovely in May when the rhododendrons are in bloom – that few people, even those who live relatively nearby, seem to know about. Situated well off the beaten track on the ridge between the Teign and Wray valleys, this is an ideal outing for anyone feeling less than energetic. Note that dogs should be kept on leads.

From the information board follow the beaten earth path away from the car park under trees. The information board provides details of various walking routes – red, orange, and green – but this walk is going to be different from all of them.

Tottiford (completed 1861, and enlarged in 1866) and Kennick (1881–3) Reservoirs were constructed to meet the growing demand for water from the increasing populations of Newton Abbot and Torquay. Trenchford followed (1903–7) as a result of an exceptional drought in 1901. The underground water pipes supplying Torquay were kept clear by the use of a 'mole' that spiralled along inside them; runners kept track of the mole from the surface, listening hard to see if it got stuck.

The path soon crosses a small wooden footbridge and runs along the edge of the water, with lovely views. Eventually, the path crosses a boardwalk, then bears right to cross the end of the reservoir on a narrow railed concrete bridge, to reach a T-junction of paths.

PUBLIC TRANSPORT None available
REFRESHMENTS None en route; picnic areas by both Trenchford and Tottiford Reservoirs; the Cleave public house in Lustleigh south west of Trenchford Reservoir
PUBLIC TOILETS None
ORDNANCE SURVEY MAPS Explorer 110 (Torquay & Dawlish), Landranger 191 (Okehampton & North Dartmoor)

A Turn left (signed Tottiford Reservoir walk). At the next T-junction of paths turn right uphill to pass through a peaceful larch plantation. This is a wonderful place; there is barely a sound as you pass over the thick carpet of needles, enjoying the resinous scent typical of such woodland. A small

Tottiford Reservoir

wooden path sign directs you left at the top of the hill along a level path, which then turns right through a spruce plantation to meet a lane at a wooden stile between granite gateposts.

B Cross the lane and over a stile; take the right fork of the two paths immediately ahead to pass to the right of a copper beech tree (signed Tottiford Reservoir). Keep straight along the main path, following an orange arrow on a post. The path runs downhill with a mossy bank and beech trees left, and conifers right, and passes through another bank. Note glimpses of Tottiford Reservoir through the tree trunks ahead.

C Turn right at the water's edge (look left to see the dam between Kennick and Tottiford Reservoirs). Follow the narrow path, which soon becomes broader and grassy, along the water's edge to reach a low, narrow, fenced bridge across the water.

D Turn left and cross the bridge. Once on the other shore, turn right and thread your way along the narrow path around the left bank

A peaceful woodland path

As well as providing great opportunities for walkers, the lakes also attract a large range of wildfowl, with heron, coot and cormorant all year round, and winter populations of **pochard, tufted duck, teal, goosander, Canada goose** and **mallard**. Kennick Reservoir also provides fishing (and is closed to walkers as a result).

of the reservoir. Just before reaching the dam, veer left through the Tottiford Reservoir picnic area to meet a lane opposite a parking area. Turn right to meet a larger tarmac lane.

E Turn left and follow the lane along the side of Trenchford Reservoir to cross the dam, from where there are great views to the left over the treatment works. Just before the dam, take a moment to look at the granite plinth and a notice through an iron gate on the right, recording the building details and opening of the reservoir. Immediately over the dam, before the lane bends sharp right, turn right through a small metal gate onto a gritty path to pass two small works buildings, the second of which marks the feeder pipe from Fernworthy Reservoir on the high moor. Follow the path to pass through the picnic area and back to the car park.   ●

? *When was the supply of water from Fernworthy introduced to Trenchford Reservoir?*

9 *Avon Dam and Rider's Rings*

START Shipley Bridge
DISTANCE 4 miles (6.4km)
TIME 2 hours
PARKING Car park (free) at Shipley Bridge (unmarked), signposted from South Brent
ROUTE FEATURES Indistinct and rough walk across open moorland from Avon Dam to Rider's Rings

The Avon is one of Dartmoor's prettiest rivers, and the stretch just above Shipley Bridge, being easily accessible, is extremely popular with visitors. But you can quickly escape: having taken the easy route to the Avon Dam, this walk strikes out across the open moor to visit a Bronze Age settlement and a particularly well-sited tor, with stunning views across the valley and over south Devon.

An ancient route commonly known as the **Abbot's Way** runs along the northern edge of the reservoir, and leads from Buckfastleigh on the south east edge of the moor to Tavistock Abbey and Buckland Abbey on the west. Its alternative name is the Jobbers' Path, dating from medieval times. Dartmoor had an important wool industry from the mid-14th to late-15th centuries, and the route is thought to have been used for collecting wool and fleeces from the southern part of the moor.

Shipley Bridge car park is on the site of the former Brent Moor china clay works, as evidenced by the ruined buildings. Clay was brought here for processing via a wooden railed tramway from Redlake china clay workings in the middle of the southern moor.

Leave the car park and turn left; just before the bridge turn left up a tarmac lane signed Brockhill Ford and Abbot's Way, with the pretty Avon on the right. The longest of southern Dartmoor's rivers at 22 miles (35km), the Avon's source is at Aune Head, a huge mire. This river is particularly lovely here, with tumbling waterfalls and deep pools.

PUBLIC TRANSPORT None available
REFRESHMENTS None en route; picnic tables near Long-a-traw; range of pubs and cafés in South Brent
PUBLIC TOILETS In car park
ORDNANCE SURVEY MAPS Explorer OL28 (Dartmoor), Landranger 202 (Torbay & South Dartmoor)

A Where a small lane leads left to the Avon Water Treatment Works, note the large block of granite – the Hunter's Stone – to the left. This is a memorial to four 19th-century South Devon Hunt masters, and was engraved by C.A. Mohun-Harris, former occupant of Brent Moor House, the crenellated gateposts of which are passed a little farther up the lane. About 50 yds (46m) beyond the gateposts there is a memorial on a rock to the left of the path, to a girl who died hereabouts in 1863. Opinions vary as to whether she drowned or died in a riding accident. The ruins of Brent Moor House are soon passed on the left. Originally the hunting lodge of the Meynell family, the house became a youth hostel before being demolished in 1968.

B The lane crosses the Avon over a bridge to enter open moorland; 250m later there is a picnic area on the right. Follow the lane as it wends its way towards the Avon Dam, which eventually can be seen ahead, blocking the valley. This part of the Avon is known as Long-a-traw, on account of its route through a moorland trough. Just before reaching the dam, the

By the Avon Dam

lane bears left to cross the river again on a granite bridge.

> **?** *What are you not allowed to do in the reservoir; and what can you do?*

C Turn left to leave the lane up a steep gritty path to reach the left end of the dam; just over the other side there is a good picnic spot at the water's edge. At times of drought the remains of a medieval farmstead may be seen on the north east side. The slopes around the reservoir are bare; most of Dartmoor's reservoirs are surrounded by plantations. The dam was built between 1955–7, to supply water to Totnes and the South Hams. Retrace your steps back to the lane.

D Walk down the lane: about 100 yds (91m) before the bridge, bear

> Larger and more remote than its more famous counterpart, Grimspound, **Rider's Rings** is an enclosed early prehistoric settlement. Divided into two areas, the remains of 34 huts and numerous enclosures have been found within the outer wall, which is believed to have been up to 10ft (3m) wide. Enclosed settlements such as this are more numerous over the more sheltered southern moor, and especially around the Erme and Avon valleys.

right over a rocky area to pick up a narrow path along the slope of a grassy plateau, avoiding a boggy area near the river. Drop down to cross Zeal Gully and stream; ahead you will see two indistinct rough paths through the bracken on the hill. Keep to the right-hand path; at the top of the hill the path levels out to meet a break in the outer wall of Rider's Rings.

E Turn right and follow the wall to its end; walk straight on and after 250 yds (228m) turn left and pick your way across a stream. Walk straight ahead, keeping high along the contours of Zeal Hill, before bearing left to Black Tor, which soon becomes visible. This is a wonderfully open, grassy route. The views from Black Tor 1,050ft (320m) are superb; look over the valley to Shipley Tor 984ft (300m), and south over the South Hams towards the sea.

F From the middle of Black Tor pick your way downhill towards the valley, towards a granite enclosure. About 20 yds from the wall bear left and follow the path downhill, parallel to the wall at first. The path descends and forks; take the right fork to reach the lane by the enclosure wall. Turn right to retrace your steps to your car. ●

Bonehill Rocks

A lovely, airy route along the tops of four impressive tors – Bonehill Rocks, Bell, Chinkwell and Honeybag Tors – overlooking the classic Dartmoor village of Widecombe in the Moor, easily recognised from countless postcards and calendars. Widecombe is a tourist honeypot, best visited on foot, and this walk offers an extension into the village via a route that largely avoids the crowds – and takes in an excellent pub.

START Just outside Widecombe in the Moor

DISTANCE 3½ miles (5.6km) with possible 1¾ mile (3.8km) extension

TIME 1¾ hours (plus 1 hour)

PARKING Marked car park (free) on the south side of the B3387 east of Widecombe

ROUTE FEATURES Rocky paths between the tors; steep walk down and back through Bonehill (extension)

? *How steep is the lane leading down from Bonehill Rocks towards Widecombe?*

Cross the road from the car park and follow the narrow path through the bracken leading directly away from the road. Almost immediately, Bonehill Rocks 1,289ft (393m) can be seen ahead and to the left. The path slopes downhill slightly and joins a wider, grassy one; keep straight on, making for the tor. A small stream

The magnificent early 16th-century tower of **St Pancras Church**, standing 135ft (41m) high, has caused it to be known as 'the cathedral of the moor'. The building of the church is said to have been funded by 'tin money'; Widecombe was, in the past, a great tin centre. The church was struck by lightning on October 21, 1638 when four of the congregation were killed, and 62 injured.

PUBLIC TRANSPORT Bus services from Exeter, Newton Abbot, Plymouth, Tavistock

REFRESHMENTS None on main route; the Rugglestone Inn, the Old Inn, Café on the Green and Wayside Café in Widecombe

PUBLIC TOILETS None on main route; in the main car park in Widecombe

PICNIC/PLAY AREA On the Natsworthy Gate lane out of Widecombe

ORDNANCE SURVEY MAPS Explorer OL28 (Dartmoor), Landranger 191 (Okehampton & North Dartmoor)

is passed as you approach the rocks. This tends to dry out in summer. There is a parking area above the path on the right. Bonehill Rocks is a great place for children, who love to explore its nooks and crannies. The views from here are stunning, and the one over Widecombe in the Moor, nearly 500ft (166m) below, is one of Dartmoor's most famous.

A Pass Bonehill Rocks and drop left downhill on the lane that runs to the right of the tor. When you reach the parking area on the left of the lane below the tor, just before a pair of granite gateposts in a wall, turn right onto a gritty track. Almost immediately, the track veers left, following a granite wall; at this point leave it and turn right uphill on an indistinct grassy path that leads to Bell Tor 1,312ft (400m), from where there are wonderful views south east to Haytor, Saddle Tor and Rippon Tor.

B Follow the grassy path north along the top of the ridge to gain the two piles of Chinkwell Tor 1,503ft (458m), the second of which is crowned by two cairns. The path then dips down

and up again to reach the various strangely-shaped rock piles of Honeybag Tor 1,460ft (445m), from which there are glorious views of the sea at Teignmouth to the south, Hound Tor to the east, and of Hamel Down over the cultivated East Webburn river valley to the west.

C Retrace your steps to the saddle between Honeybag and Chinkwell Tors, and cross the embanked gully. William Crossing noted a line of manorial boundary stones here, in the region marked 'Slades Well', and there are remains of Bronze Age hut circles, too. Turn right down a broad grassy path that leads off the ridge to meet a gritty track, formerly a carriage drive. Turn left and follow the level track to reach the lane by Bonehill Rocks.

D To return to your car, cross straight over the lane and through the lower edge of the car park to pass below the tor. Cross over the stream at the far side of the tor to rejoin the grassy path below the parking area. About 100 yds (91m) later the path dips down; just before it crosses a large slab of granite, veer left on a narrow path through the bracken to reach the road opposite the car park.

Bonehill Rocks

Note: If you feel like a drink at the Rugglestone Inn, turn right at **D** *and walk steeply downhill through the peaceful hamlet at Bonehill. At the end lane end turn left and immediately right over a stile (signed public footpath); at the end of that field cross a wooden stile and iron railings and turn left; the pub is within 100 yds (91m). The Rugglestone has a pretty garden, with a stream. After lunch, walk straight back along the lane into the village past the church, 15th-century Church House and Sexton's Cottage (NT). A shop and information centre can be found in the Church House. Turn right along the road opposite the 14th-century Old Inn, to pass the green, and take the next lane left to retrace your steps up the hill to reach point* **D** *again, by Bonehill Rocks.* ●

Widecombe Fair, originally an important livestock market, is today a highly commercialised affair, held on the second Tuesday of September. The popular ballad woven around the story of 'Uncle Tom Cobley 'n' all' tells of how Tom Pearce's grey mare made her way to Widecombe Fair carrying six individuals, and was (not surprisingly) ridden to her death. She is said to haunt the local moor to this day. The event is commemorated in relief on the granite parish sign near the village green.

11 *Crazywell Pool*

START Norsworthy Bridge, signposted from Burrator Reservoir dam
DISTANCE 3½ miles (5.6km)
TIME 2 hours
PARKING Parking area (free) near Norsworthy Bridge
ROUTE FEATURES Steep rocky downhill path to the River Meavy

A wonderfully varied walk, starting and ending through the peaceful forest plantations around Burrator Reservoir. The middle section crosses the open moor and takes in mysterious Crazywell Pool, home to a wealth of legends, before following the Devonport Leat as it tumbles down Raddick Hill to cross the Meavy river on a little aqueduct.

There are various parking spaces around Norsworthy Bridge; park in the main one as indicated on the map. Walk towards the bridge, over the stream.

A As the lane bends sharp left to cross the bridge turn right up a rough wooded track, with lovely old granite walls. After a few

> **?** *Which three animal footprints are represented in colour on the wooden posts found near the start and end of the walk?*

minutes a T-junction of tracks is reached; Norsworthy Plantation is to the left. Turn right, to follow the track slightly uphill and along the edge of the plantation. Views of Down Tor 1,135ft (346m) open up to the right. At the next junction of paths, Raddick Lane joins from the left; keep walking right on the main track. The trees of Raddick Plantation gradually become thinner as the track reaches a wooden gate that leads onto the open moor. Newleycombe Lake (the valley below right) has a wealth of old tin-mining remains.

PUBLIC TRANSPORT None available
REFRESHMENTS None en route; Royal Oak pub at Meavy south west of Burrator Reservoir; many good picnic spots around Burrator Reservoir
PUBLIC TOILETS None en route; by reservoir dam
ORDNANCE SURVEY MAPS Explorer OL28 (Dartmoor), Landranger 202 (Torbay & South Dartmoor)

B Once through the gate, look back for great views over Burrator Reservoir, which covers 150 acres (60.75ha) and was constructed from 1891–8 to supply water to Plymouth. Enlarged in 1928, it has a capacity of 1,026 million gallons (4,572 million litres), and replaced Drake's Leat. The surrounding forests were first planted in 1921. Continue up the track; where a spring crosses the path turn left up a narrow path onto grassy moorland, just to the right of a deep gully. Note a restored stone cross on the horizon ahead and slightly to the right. Follow the gully and within a few minutes Crazywell Pool is reached.

C Skirt around the right edge of

Crazywell Pool is a flooded mineworking, but its remote location has given rise to all kinds of legends and superstitions. Some believe it to be tidal, linked to the sea at Plymouth by a huge tunnel; some think it is bottomless; but the most eerie tale relates to a wailing voice that calls out the name of the next person to die in the parish of Walkhampton...and on Midsummer's Eve the reflection of that person can be seen in the dark waters of the pool.

the pool, then walk straight ahead from the top corner across the moor towards some blocks of dressed granite, which are lying just by the Devonport Leat. Cross the leat over the stone slab bridge.

Aqueduct on the Devonport Leat

D Turn left and follow the leat along its right bank, passing two more stone slab bridges and a sluice gate, used to divert water out of the leat if the flow was too heavy. This path is boggy in places, and becomes rockier as the steep descent off Raddick Hill is made. Follow the leat as it rushes down to cross the River Meavy on a small aqueduct, built in 1792. The path leads over metal rails at each end of the aqueduct. As the leat bends sharp left, note the feeder pipe bringing in water from the Hart Tor Brook. The Meavy valley to the right here is rich in Bronze Age and tin-working remains; this is a great picnic spot.

E Follow the leat on, keeping to the right bank: a level and very easy walk after clambering over the open moor. The leat loops left to pass under the wall of Stanlake Plantation. Note the ruins of

Stanlake Farm on the left; there are many deserted farms in the feeder valleys of the reservoir. Turn left at the wall, then right over a stile into the plantation (signed Crossgate and Yennadon). The leat is wonderfully quiet here, and the forest light and open; see if you can spot any brown trout in the waters. At the next junction of paths, Leather Tor Farm is signed right; keep walking straight on along the leat. The clitter of Leather Tor (1,181ft/360m) is visible through the mixed deciduous trees to the right. The path drops down and over a stile by double gates.

F Just past the stile, turn left downhill to leave the leat (although it is very tempting to keep following it at this point). The next footpath sign directs you left for Norsworthy Bridge down a narrow path that crosses a track; then over a wooden stile and downhill through recently planted trees. The path ends at a wooden stile onto the lane; turn left to cross Norsworthy Bridge and back to the car.

●

The East and West Okement Rivers

12

START Okehampton
DISTANCE 4½ miles (7.2km)
TIME 2¾ hours
PARKING Fee-paying car park in Mill Road, off East Street, Okehampton
ROUTE FEATURES Occasionally rocky and narrow path by East Okement river; short yet steep climb through Halstock Wood

The old market town of Okehampton on the northern fringe of Dartmoor (bypassed by the A30) is full of surprises. Within minutes of leaving the town you enter the lovely wooded valley of the East Okement river; then cross farmland overlooking Dartmoor's highest tors before descending through beech woods surrounding romantic Okehampton castle.

Leave the car park via the entrance, and turn right. Where the lane bends sharp right, fork left onto a narrow tarmac lane, with an old mill on the corner, following signs for Ball Hill and East Okement valley. This is part of the 90-mile (145km) Dartmoor Way, and also the Tarka Trail, which runs for 180 miles (290km) from Okehampton to the north coast and Exmoor. Follow the lane (with a leat on the left) to its end by

Okehampton Castle is the largest castle in Devon, and was built by the Norman sheriff of Devon, Baldwin de Brionne, soon after 1066, although much of what remains today dates from the 13th and 15th centuries. The castle has been used as a strategic garrison over the centuries, and encouraged the development of Okehampton as an important market town for the area. For many generations it was owned by the Courtenay family, one time Earls of Devon, and today is under the care of English Heritage.

? *What animal paw print is used to mark the route of the Tarka Trail, and why?*

PUBLIC TRANSPORT Bus services from Barnstaple, Exeter, Newton Abbot, Plymouth, Torquay, Totnes
REFRESHMENTS Good range of pubs and cafés in Okehampton
PUBLIC TOILETS In car park
ORDNANCE SURVEY MAPS Explorer OL28 (Dartmoor), Landranger 191 (Okehampton & North Dartmoor)

Okehampton College playing fields' car park.

A Walk through a five-bar gate; follow the path through three fields/three kissing-gates to reach a gritty track coming in from the left. Walk through a five-bar gate to enter Ball Hill conservation area. This is a beautiful wooded path – note the leat and sluice gate by the stream on the right – and ends at a five-bar gate onto a lane.

B Turn right; pass Moorcot (right); go through a gate, under the

railway viaduct, then turn right over the stream via a wooden bridge, and the East Okement River via a railed wooden bridge. Turn left through a five-bar gate, following signs for the East Okement valley, and under the A30 viaduct. Keep on the right bank of the river, signed Chapel Ford and

The East Okement River

the moor. The river is a delight, tumbling over granite boulders and providing excellent picnic spots; the intrusive A30 is quickly left behind. The path crosses granite stepping stones (wet in winter), and crosses a stream to enter West Cleave. Pass through an old granite wall to regain the river where it runs narrowly through broad granite pavements. Continue along the right bank; at a waterfall, the route climbs steeply over a rocky outcrop before dropping downhill.

C Before reaching Chapel Ford turn sharp right uphill through Halstock Wood by a footpath post. The path meets a stock fence and runs right through bracken and hazel, with great views right. Pass through a five-bar gate and granite gateposts, and on through bracken and rowan above the wooded Moor Brook valley (right). A bank/fence comes in from the left; keep it on the left and proceed to a signpost.

D Turn right downhill; pick your way down to the Moor Brook, and over the stepping stones. Turn left along a narrow path through woodland and over a stile; cross the next stile into a field. Keep

The **London and South Western Railway** line reached Okehampton in 1871. The line was extended on to Lydford in 1874 via the Meldon viaduct, climbing to 950ft (290m) above sea level at Prewley summit en route (the highest point on any Southern Region railway system), and on to Tavistock in 1876. The line closed for passengers in 1968, and today the Dartmoor Railway runs trains as far as the viaduct, which is now open for walkers and cyclists only.

along the right edge (wall) and pass through a gate onto a lane. Turn right up the lane, which leads up along the edge of East Hill, with great views of Dartmoor's highest tors, and the army camp, built in the early 1880s. The army has used Dartmoor for training since the Napoleonic wars in the early 19th century, and now uses about one third of the open moor. The lane ends at a cattle-grid by a lane.

Okehampton Castle ruins

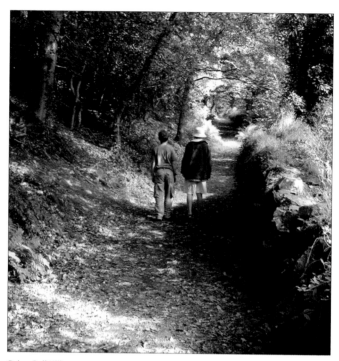

Below Ball Hill

E Turn right; follow the road downhill over the A30 and railway; Okehampton Castle can be seen among the trees ahead. As the houses are reached, turn left along Tors Road (signed 'to the golf course'), following signs to Meldon viaduct. Pass through a gate by a cattle-grid and enter beech woods; turn right downhill, signed 'castle and Okehampton'. The path drops down to cross the West Okement River via a double railed footbridge and wall to enter the castle car park.

F Turn left for the castle. For the car, turn right along Castle Road, passing the hospital and Brock's Almshouses (1847). At the end of the lane, cross the road and turn right in front of Fairplace church. Pass Simmons Park and Okehampton College on the right; follow the road past the old mill; retrace your steps down Mill Road to the car park. ●

Foggintor and Swelltor Quarries

13

START Just west of Princetown

DISTANCE 3½ miles (5.6 km)

TIME 1½ hours

PARKING Parking area (free) just off track to Yellowmeade Farm, on the B3357

ROUTE FEATURES Brief rocky scramble around the edge of a gully at Swelltor Quarry

Nearly 200 years ago this rather remote part of the moor was buzzing with industrial activity, brought about by one man's ultimately misguided dream of creating a prosperous community at Princetown. The walk follows part of the line of the old iron railway, opened in 1823, linking Princetown with Plymouth.

🖊 Walk away from the road down the gritty track, signed

There are clear views of **Merrivale Quarry** from the old railway line. Originally known as Tor Quarry, this operated from 1875 to 1997, and was the last working quarry on Dartmoor. Granite blocks from the old London Bridge were re-dressed here when the bridge was sold to the USA, and stone was also used in the war memorial in the Falklands after the war in 1982. Watch out for the famous prehistoric Merrivale stone rows on the valley slopes as you look across to the quarry.

Yellowmeade Farm (private road). Look ahead and, to the right, pick out the line of the old railway line as it runs beneath King's Tor 1,263ft (385m), and large spoil heaps ahead, indicating the edge of Foggintor granite quarries. As Yellowmeade Farm is approached, take the track that runs left of the farmhouse, and follow that to reach the edge of Foggintor Quarries.

Ⓐ Swelltor and Foggintor Quarries operated from around

PUBLIC TRANSPORT Bus service (to Princetown) from Exeter, Newton Abbot, Plymouth, Tavistock, Totnes

REFRESHMENTS None en route; pubs and cafés in Princetown; also the Dartmoor Inn at Merrivale just west on the B3357

PUBLIC TOILETS None en route

ORDNANCE SURVEY MAPS Explorer OL28 (Dartmoor), Landranger 191 (Okehampton & North Dartmoor)

1820, in direct competition with George Templer's quarries at Haytor. Fogginton (originally known as Royal Oak Quarry)

ceased working around 1900, and Swelltor in 1921, although both quarries reopened in 1937 in response to an increase in demand for road building materials. Fogginton supplied granite for Dartmoor prison, and local granite was used in Nelson's Column in Trafalgar Square. There are masses of ruined buildings to the side of

The **Plymouth and Dartmoor Railway** was the brainchild of Sir Thomas Tyrwhitt, and ran for just over 25 miles (40km) across the moors and through farmland. A friend of and private secretary to the Prince Regent, he was responsible for the development of Princetown, the building of the prison, and the railway (actually a tramway, with horse-drawn wagons). After the Napoleonic wars granite was much in demand for building works, and Tyrwhitt seized the opportunity to exploit the area's natural resources, at the same time enabling materials such as coal and lime to be brought to Princetown more easily. The Princetown Railway Company (subsidiary of the GWR) took over the line in 1881; it reopened as a steam railway in 1883, but was never profitable and closed in 1956.

What do you think the 12 blocks of dressed granite lying by the track near King's Tor might have been used for?

the quarries here, including (on the right of the path) the site of a chapel, also used as a school. Walk left down the narrow cleft that leads to the flooded quarry: it is wonderfully peaceful and sheltered, and a great picnic spot. Returning to the main track, continue walking through the workings, keeping the quarry on the left. At the end of the quarry there are views to the sea at Plymouth Sound ahead.

Pool at Swelltor Quarry

B As the track curves left, turn right and follow the path over the disused embanked railway track (near the site of King Tor Halt, dating from 1928, from where a siding called Royal Oak led to Foggintor). Walk ahead up the grassy path; this is crossed by two tracks, both of which are visible as you approach them. Turn left on the first of these and follow it along the contours of the hill to gain Swelltor Quarries, where the path ends at a deep gully and spoil heaps; *pick your way carefully around the right edge of this.*

C Pick up the quarry siding on the other side, and follow this easy, level route around the contours of the hill towards King's Tor. The track reaches an area of ruined buildings and old workings by King's Tor Quarry, overlooking the wooded valley of the River Walkham, with great views of Vixen Tor 1,024ft (312m) beyond. Thought to be home to one of the moor's most evil characters, the witch Vixana, Vixen Tor is the tallest tor on Dartmoor, standing almost 100ft (30m) high. Note the grass-covered wooden sleepers on the track. Just after the quarry you will come across 12 corbels lying at the side of the track, which then drops gently down to meet the disused Plymouth and Dartmoor railway line.

D Follow the old line around the hill, and over a high embankment with a granite bridge beneath. Follow this easy, elevated line until it reaches the point at which it was crossed on the outward route **B**; turn left uphill to regain the track at Foggintor Quarries. Turn left and retrace your steps to the car. ●

14 *Scorhill*

START Moor gate at Scorhill

DISTANCE 4½ miles (7.2km)

TIME 2¼ hours

PARKING Unmarked parking area (free) at end of lane; Scorhill is signposted from Gidleigh

ROUTE FEATURES Rough moorland for first half of walk; steep woodland path down to River Teign and back up through Gidleigh Woods

This varied walk is full of natural and man-made features that span many thousands of years: stone circles, clapper bridges, a tolmen stone, one of the deepest rock basins on a Dartmoor tor, Bronze Age and Iron Age settlements, a medieval path that crossed the whole of Devon, an ancient church and a ruined castle.

Scorhill stone circle is nearly 90ft (27.5m) in diameter and comprises more than 30 stones, the tallest around 8ft (2.5m) high, and probably dates from the early Bronze Age. Many similar circles on the moor have been restored, but Scorhill has not, although some stones have been removed and used to line the leat a little farther downhill. Dartmoor has a wealth of Bronze Age remains, and the many standing stones, stone circles and stone rows are thought to have some kind of ritual significance.

Walk through the wooden gate onto the moor, and uphill on the broad grassy path. Where the granite wall to the left veers off left keep straight on up the slightly sunken path. As you reach the crest of the hill Kestor Rock can be seen ahead and left, beyond the conifers fringing Batworthy. As you descend, the path splits; keep right to reach Scorhill stone circle.

Ⓐ Turn left at the circle and walk downhill, aiming for the point at which the conifers drop into the valley of the Teign river. En route, the path crosses a small leat; nearer the river the way becomes rocky and uneven, but leads directly to

PUBLIC TRANSPORT None available

REFRESHMENTS None en route; Northmore Arms at Wonson north of Gidleigh; several pubs and cafés in Chagford

PUBLIC TOILETS None en route

ORDNANCE SURVEY MAPS Explorer OL28 (Dartmoor), Landranger 191 (Okehampton & North Dartmoor)

the Tolmen Stone, a large granite block with a hole through it, caused by water erosion. The stone is lodged high above the river, shifted from its original position during a time of flood. Crawling through such a hole was once thought to cure rheumatism, or whooping cough in children – and many people venture through the Tolmen Stone today – just in case.

B Turn right and walk up river, then left over the Walla Brook clapper bridge, then over the Teign on Teign-e-ver clapper bridge. Walk straight ahead uphill, keeping the wall and conifers around Batworthy on your left; parts of this can be muddy. Follow the wall until it bends very sharply left; as you round the corner, Kestor Rock 1,434ft (437m) is directly ahead. Clamber to the top of the rocks, from where there are fantastic views in all directions. Look for the water-filled rock basin on the top, which, when cleared out in 1856, was railed off to prevent sheep from drowning. Thought to be the deepest such basin on the moor (and a natural feature), in Victorian times it was said to be used to catch blood from those unfortunates sacrificed by Druids.

ⓒ From Kestor turn left and walk along the top of the ridge, with wooded Batworthy to the left, and a wall and woodland in the valley right. This leads you through the area of Bronze Age and later Iron Age settlement, originating from around 1500BC. At the end of the

There is extensive evidence of **Bronze Age** and **Iron Age** occupation to the north of **Kestor Rock**, in the form of field systems (reaves – field boundaries) and hut circles. Iron Age remains are unusual on the moor; climatic deterioration before that time caused much of it to become depopulated, but cultivation continued at this site on the drier, eastern side. Near the lane (see map) there is a round pound, possibly a smithy, dating from around 500BC, with the remains of a hut within its own enclosure.

ridge drop down left to meet a lane, and turn right downhill through a gate by a cattle-grid.

ⓓ Around 100 yds (91m) along the lane turn left down a rough track, signed Gidleigh, and over a stile. At the bottom of the hill the path is signed right, then left very steeply downhill through a coniferous plantation to meet the Teign at Glassy Steps, which is crossed via a double-railed wooden footbridge. This is on the route of the Mariner's Way, a possible medieval

Kestor Rock

The Tolmen Stone

track that ran from Dartmouth, on the south coast, to Bideford on the north. Once over the river you meet a track; follow the signs right through North Park (part of Gidleigh Woods). The next path sign directs you sharp left and steeply uphill; as the conifers thin out at the top the path levels off and crosses a gritty area; follow the signs along a track between granite walls to meet a lane at a gate and stile.

E Turn right downhill, and left at the next junction (Gidleigh Cross) by Gidleigh village hall. Walk on to find 15th-century Gidleigh church – Holy Trinity – a very pretty, simple granite building, with a wonderful line of 17th-/18th-century headstones against the outer wall. The graveyard is a carpet of snowdrops in February. Just beyond the church look through the iron gates of Gidleigh Castle, a fortified manor house built by Sir William Prous around AD1300. The ruined keep can be seen clearly; now privately owned, it is occasionally open to the public. Follow the lane uphill to a T-junction; turn left uphill, then left again (signed Creaber and Scorhill). Where the lane bends sharp left (signed Gidleigh and Berrydown) turn right opposite Cherryford House and walk up the lane to the car park. ●

> **?** *Find the west window in the church. In whose memory was it restored?*

15 The Dewerstone

START Cadover Bridge

DISTANCE 3¾ miles (6km)

TIME 2 hours

PARKING Car park (free) at Cadover Bridge

ROUTE FEATURES Steep, rocky descent towards Dewerstone Crags; uneven, narrow path through North Wood

This is a popular walk that can easily be done in either direction. There is a mass of interest here: the Plym at Cadover Bridge is great for paddling and picnics; Shaugh Bridge is a popular beauty spot; there are usually climbers tackling the famous Dewerstone Crags; and there is also a wealth of fascinating industrial archaeological remains.

The wooded Plym Valley

Walk towards Cadover Bridge along the riverbank, and cross the river via the bridge. Walk a little way up the road, then turn left across the grass just before you reach granite posts on either side of the road, and a gritty track on the left. Aim for the granite cross that you will see ahead of you and slightly uphill.

Ⓐ Standing over 6½ft (2m) high, Cadover Cross sits on an ancient route linking Plympton and

> **?** *There is an inscription on the top of Dewerstone Rock. Can you make out the name of the person whose memorial this is?*

PUBLIC TRANSPORT None available

REFRESHMENTS Ice cream van in car parks at Cadover Bridge and Shaugh Bridge; Royal Oak pub at Meavy north west of Cadover Bridge

PUBLIC TOILETS None en route

ORDNANCE SURVEY MAPS Explorer OL28 (Dartmoor), Landranger 202 (Torbay & South Dartmoor)

Tavistock. It was re-erected in 1873, but fell again and was restored by the Reverend Hugh Breton, vicar of Sheepstor, in 1915, and set in a large socket stone. Walk uphill away from the cross, keeping the granite wall on the left. Where the wall turns left, follow it round and walk along the open, grassy ridge of Wigford Down. There are Bronze Age hut circles and cairns in the area, dating from around 1000BC. Follow the line of the ridge past Oxen Tor; the path dips down and up again to reach Dewerstone Rock 745ft (227m), crossing a line of Iron Age fortifications on the way, with wonderful views of the Plym valley to the left.

Plymouth Sound is visible from the top of the rock.

B Turn left from the rock and pick your way steeply downhill towards the wooded valley of the Plym. The path crosses a broken-down granite wall then falls steeply through oak woodland to reach the

The **Dewerstone Crags** have many associations with the Devil, whose hounds are believed to round up unrepentant sinners and force them over the edge of the crags. It is also said that the woods here are haunted by an enormous evil red-eyed dog. The Devil is, not surprisingly, known locally as 'Dewer'.

top of the Dewerstone Crags. Look for a path leading away right through the woods, and follow that path along the side of the hill. Where it meets a gritty track, turn left and zigzag down through the trees. The track here has been restored; this area, known as Goodameavy, is an SSSI and is in the care of the National Trust. At the end of the track cross the Plym just above Shaugh Bridge (late 1820s) on a gated wooden footbridge, then take the path (left) into the car park. The Plym and Meavy Rivers meet at this point.

C Look out for the drying kilns in the car park; from now on the route is peppered with evidence of the old china clay industry. Before reaching the road turn left up steep stone steps to leave the car park, and follow the path above the road, signed for Cadover Bridge. Look out for the remains of an old

settling tank to the left of the path, just before crossing a wooden stile. The path runs steeply uphill (muddy in winter), then broadens and becomes more open, with good views to the right. At the next split in the path (a modern house is to the right), keep left under the trees; very soon the first piece of pipeline can be seen, half-buried under the surface of the path. Pass another settling tank on the left, after which the path levels and leads through light oak, ash, birch and rowan woodland. Across the Plym valley to the left are great views of the Dewerstone Crags.

D Follow the path over a stile into North Wood (NT), still looking out for evidence of the pipe. This is beautiful oak wood-land, with areas of soft green grass and the pretty, rocky River Plym below to the left; there are lots of good places for picnics and toe-dipping. Follow the path over a wooden footbridge and stile, across the corner of a field, then up a wooden ladder over a wall and back into woodland. The path eventually leaves the wood via a slightly boggy plantation of willows, then over a stile and into the car park. ●

The Plym above Shaugh Bridge

Wistman's Wood

16

If you want to escape from any signs of civilisation within a few minutes of leaving your car, this is the walk for you. A rough track leads to Wistman's Wood, a magical ancient upland oak woodland, from where you set out across open moorland to cross the West Dart river on stepping stones, before an easy return along the banks of the Devonport Leat.

START Two Bridges Hotel
DISTANCE 4½ miles (7.2km)
TIME 2½ hours
PARKING Parking area (free) opposite the Two Bridges Hotel just west of the B3212/3357 junction
ROUTE FEATURES Rough, open moorland beyond Wistman's Wood; river crossing on granite boulders; *do not attempt this walk after very heavy rainfall*

From the car park pass through the gate (signed Wistman's Wood) and follow the broad, stony track, which ends at Crockern Tor Farm; pass to the right of the farm over a rocky path to reach a footpath post, and the first view of Wistman's Wood ahead, nestling on the right bank of the West Dart River.

A Follow the track on; a small path soon leads off right towards Crockern Tor 1,312ft (400m). The track continues through a granite wall, then drops down and becomes sandy. Look across the

Equidistant from the stannary towns of Ashburton, Chagford, Plympton and Tavistock, and at the centre of Dartmoor's tin-mining areas, **Crockern Tor** is famous as the ancient site of the Great Court, the stannary parliament where tin-mining representatives met to regulate the industry. One natural rock formation does indeed resemble a giant chair, and is known as the Parliament Rock or Judge's Chair. The first records of the Great Court date from 1474, although meetings could have been held earlier. The last meeting (in Moretonhampstead) was held in 1786.

valley to spot the Devonport Leat. Cross a ladder-stile at the boundary

PUBLIC TRANSPORT Bus service from Exeter, Plymouth, Tavistock and Totnes
REFRESHMENTS The Two Bridges Hotel, also at Crockern Tor Farm (seasonal)
PUBLIC TOILETS None en route; at the Two Bridges Hotel
ORDNANCE SURVEY MAPS Explorer OL28 (Dartmoor), Landranger 191 (Okehampton & North Dartmoor)

of Crockern Tor and Longaford Newtakes, and go on across open grassy moorland to reach Wistman's Wood. This extraordinary and atmospheric place is said to be a favoured haunt of the Devil's hounds, which round up sinners and drive them into the dense woodland, from where they never escape.

B Pick your way carefully up and along the top edge of the wood. The path is bouldery and indistinct. Pass the last two or three clumps of oaks, and keep straight on; this part of the route is over uneven, open moorland.

Wistman's Wood (NNR) is one of only three remaining areas of ancient upland oak woodland on the moor, the others being Piles Copse, on the Erme, and Blackator Copse, on the West Okement River. It is an enchanting place: the twisted, stunted oaks, growing from a bed of moss-covered boulders (which have protected them from destructive grazing) are festooned with tree ferns and lichens, many of which can survive here because of the lack of air pollution.

Look right to see Longaford Tor 1,663ft (507m), below which is the site of a mid-to-late 19th-century gunpowder factory. Walk on, keeping along the contours rather than dropping down to the river, where the land is boggy. Look ahead and left, towards the head weir of the leat and a green hut on the opposite bank,

En route for Wistman's Wood

and you will see a ladder-stile on this side of the river; aim for the stile.

C Cross the stile. You can cross the river at the weir (built in the 1790s) – at low water only – or turn left and cross it on large boulders about 50 yds (46m) down river, where a big flat rock juts out from the bank. Scramble up the opposite bank to find the 27-mile (43km) long Devonport Leat, an amazing feat of late 18th-century engineering (for more details see Crazywell Pool, Walk 11). It provides a very attractive, level route high above the West Dart, enhanced by the combined sounds of its own tinkling waters and the rushing river below. Follow the narrow path along the left bank of

the leat around the contours of Beardown Hill, crossing one stile en route, towards a coniferous plantation. Just before the woodland, climb around two small granite walls by a concrete bridge, and continue along the leat to enter the wood over a stile.

D Follow the path along the left bank through the dark conifers to emerge over a stile, then cross another stile, now surrounded by fields. Cross over another stile to reach a track. Turn left to leave the leat; walk downhill to reach the edge of Beardown Farm. At the farmyard follow the footpath sign

> **?** *How many stone slab bridges can you count crossing the Devonport Leat?*

right over a stile and down the track, with a line of beech trees on the left. The track joins another at a T-junction; turn right to cross the Cowsic River, following the footpath sign. Just over the bridge follow the footpath sign left, and clamber down steeply to walk along the right bank of the river. Cross another stile, and continue above the rushing river; then over a stile and along the bottom of small field. Leave the field over a ladder up a granite bank, then a stile and footbridge, and across the next field. Over a stile, along a grassy track, and over a stile to gain the road just west of the Two Bridges Hotel.

Cross the road with care and turn left down the old lane over the second of the two bridges into the hotel car park; turn left and cross over the road to return to the car park.

Wistman's Wood – a place of secrets

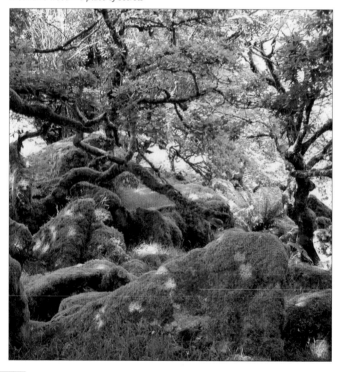

Dr Blackall's Drive

The views from this walk must be some of the loveliest and most wide-ranging on Dartmoor. The route follows a scenic carriageway above the deeply-incised Dart valley, then runs through woods and farmland to reach the tiny hamlets of Leusdon and Ponsworthy, before a final stretch across beautiful open moorland.

17

START Bel Tor Corner, north west of Poundsgate
DISTANCE 5¼ miles (8.4km)
TIME 2½ hours
PARKING Unsurfaced car park (free) at Bel Tor Corner, on the Ashburton–Dartmeet road
ROUTE FEATURES Steep ascent up the lane from the River Dart and through Park Wood; also up the lane from Lower Town to Leusdon church

🥾 Walk straight ahead from the car park (on the Two Moors Way), keeping the granite wall and Bel Tor on the left (inaccessible to the public). Sharp Tor 1,214ft (370m) lies ahead and to the right, just to the south west of which are the remains of Vaghill Warren, one of several sources of rabbit meat during Dartmoor's tin-mining boom. Venford Reservoir, built

Cottage near Leusdon

between 1901 and 1907 to supply water to Paignton, can be seen ahead across the valley of the Dart; the workers lived on site and were paid the princely sum of 12s (60p) a week, a good wage in those days.

Ⓐ The path turns left along a walled track; follow it as it veers left again just before Mel Tor 1,135ft (346m). Up until the 1950s

---

PUBLIC TRANSPORT Bus service from Tavistock and Totnes
REFRESHMENTS Mobile refreshments in the car park; picnic area by the River Dart; the Tavistock Inn at Poundsgate (not en route)
PUBLIC TOILETS None en route
ORDNANCE SURVEY MAPS Explorer OL28 (Dartmoor), Landrangers 191 (Okehampton & North Dartmoor) and 202 (Torbay & South Dartmoor)

a local custom was played out here. This involved rolling wagon wheels down the slopes of the tor to see if any could reach the river. The path drops down and veers left to run above the deeply wooded and very beautiful Dart valley. This is the line of Dr Blackall's Drive, the views from which are glorious.

Follow the level, grassy track, round Aish Tor. Just past a fenced-off quarry (right) bear right

Scenic carriage drives were all the rage among wealthy landowners in the 19th century. During the 1870s, **Dr Joseph Blackall**, who lived at 17th-century Spitchwick Manor, had one laid out above the spectacular Dart valley for his personal enjoyment. 'Dr Blackall's Drive' crosses the Poundsgate–Dartmeet road near the top of the hill above Spitchwick, and provides a very easy walking route today.

Looking towards Buckland from Leusdon church

downhill on a broad grassy path, to reach a track. Turn left to reach a lane. Cross the lane and keep ahead to meet the road.

B Cross the road (small parking area) and follow the narrow path ahead to pass to the left of Leigh Tor. The path continues downhill to meet the edge of Park Wood; turn right and drop downhill to meet the lane opposite the River Dart. (If you want to break for a picnic here, turn right to find a lovely grassy picnic area on the banks of the river.)

C Turn left to pass Spitchwick Lower Lodge on the left. Note the old metal suspension bridge (locked) over the river on the right. Just past that, turn left up a steep lane, signed Lower Town. Where the lane bends sharp right to cross

a stream, turn left up a woodland track, signed Poundsgate. The track runs steeply up through Park Wood to a gate and stile at the top, to enter fields; follow the path, keeping the hedge on the right, to reach a five-bar gate by a pond (right). Go through the gate and along the bottom of the next field, through a five-bar gate and another field, then through a gate onto a lane on a bend; Spitchwick Manor gardens are over the wall opposite.

D Turn right and follow the lane past Brick Cottage on the left. Just past the cottage turn right, following a path sign through a small wooden gate into a field. Keeping the hedge on the left, walk down the field to reach two gates. Go through the gate on the right and through the next field, with the hedge left; through another gate, along the next field and through a gate to reach Lower Town, part of the hamlet of Leusdon ('Leofwine's farm'). The narrow, gritty track joins the lane.

E Turn left to pass Town Farm and walk up the steep hill to find the church of St John the Baptist on the right, the building of which, in 1863, was funded by Charlotte Rosamund Larpent. A stained glass window in the west wall of the

The tower of **St Peter's Church** at **Buckland** can be seen from Leusdon. The church clock is unusual in that, instead of numerals, it displays the words MY DEAR MOTHER, the creation of a local landowner who was also responsible for the carving of the Ten Commandments stone on top of Buckland Beacon 1,247ft (380m) in 1928. A second carved rock nearby commemorates the silver jubilee of King George V in 1935. The beacon originates from the time of the Spanish Armada.

church commemorates her work, and the church replaced the Chapel of St Leonard, at Spitchwick. There are fantastic views towards Buckland Beacon and church from the churchyard. Walk on uphill; the lane levels off to pass a small lane on the left, and meets the tarmac road. Turn right and follow the road downhill into Ponsworthy.

F Turn left at Forder Bridge, where there is a small ford. Ponsworthy lies on a medieval packhorse route from Tavistock to Bovey Tracey, and the current Ponsworthy Bridge, which crosses the West Webburn River in the centre of the hamlet, bears the date 1666. The bridge is said to have been crossed by the Devil on a black horse during the great storm of Widecombe in 1638, on which day he also dropped in at the Tavistock Inn at

> *On what date did Mrs Larpent, founder of Leusdon church, die, and how old was she?*

Poundsgate, where the money he left in payment later mysteriously turned to leaves... Follow the lane steeply uphill; at the junction of lanes at the top (Lock's Gate Cross) go straight on, signed Dartmeet. After 50 yds (46m) turn left on a disused unmarked grassy track (the Two Moors Way). Just before Primm Cottage, bear right off the track. Bear slightly left as the top of the paddock behind the cottage is passed; on a broad grassy path, and continue uphill to reach the road opposite the car park.   ●

On Dr Blackall's Drive

Fernworthy and Grey Wethers

18

A chance to experience the desolate wilds of deserted Teignhead Farm and the upper North Teign River, barely a mile from its source, and to visit the largest stone circles on the moor, via a wealth of attractive and varied woodland paths through Fernworthy Forest and around Fernworthy Reservoir.

START Fernworthy Reservoir

DISTANCE 5¼ miles (8.4km)

TIME 2¼ hours

PARKING Car park (free) at Fernworthy Reservoir, signposted from Chagford

ROUTE FEATURES Rough indistinct track across open moor from forest edge to Grey Wethers; dogs to be kept under close control around the reservoir (breeding birds)

In 1927 Torquay Corporation was authorised to extract water from the South Teign River, which now runs from the dam to join the North Teign at Leigh Bridge, near Chagford. The Teign (the name comes from the old dialect for river, 'ta') reaches the sea at Teignmouth. By 1929 a weir had been built, with an intake and pipeline running to **Trenchford Reservoir**; the Prince of Wales (the future King Edward VIII) visited the site in 1930.

Leave the car park with the toilets on the left; the information board supplies useful facts on wildflowers and wildlife. Pass through a bank onto a track and turn right. Look right towards the dam; increased demand for water for the growing population of Torbay led to Torquay Corporation being given authority to build a reservoir here, to dam the South Teign river, in 1934. Construction started in August 1936, and the 380-million gallon (1,729-litre) reservoir was opened in June 1942 at a cost of £246,000. There were originally three farms at Fernworthy, referred to as a 'village' in the 17th century, and in times of drought the old clapper

PUBLIC TRANSPORT None available

REFRESHMENTS Mobile café sometimes in car park; picnic area near car park; good range of pubs and cafés in Chagford

PUBLIC TOILETS In car park

ORDNANCE SURVEY MAPS Explorer OL28 (Dartmoor), Landranger 191 (Okehampton & North Dartmoor)

bridge over the South Teign emerges from the bed of the reservoir.

A Follow the gritty track towards the reservoir. At the next footpath post turn left along a bark-chip path through the conifers, with good views of Thornworthy Tor 1,391ft (424m) across the water. This pretty path undulates through silver birch and rowan trees to reach another footpath post; go straight on (signed 'bird hide walk') to cross a double-railed footbridge and enter a grassy area. Turn right, then bear left at the next footpath post and walk up the grassy slope to pass a bird hide (with disabled access) on the right. Pass through the wooden gate to leave the Wildlife Protection Area. Walk straight on to join a track; turn right to reach the tarmac lane.

B Turn right; follow the lane as it curves around the south west tip of the reservoir and crosses a granite bridge. The lane ends at a small parking area. Turn left up a gritty track, signed 'to moor', which runs gradually uphill; at the next fork keep left. As the track drops downhill look right to see a small Bronze Age double stone row and stone circle in a clearing. Fernworthy Forest was planted from 1919 to 1936, originally to replenish timber supplies after the First World War, and then to enhance the scenic qualities of the reservoir. Fernworthy is

Dartmoor's largest forest, covering almost 1,500 acres (680ha), and the swathes of Sitka spruce, Japanese larch and Douglas fir provide a wealth of walking and cycling opportunities. Keep on the track; at a crossroads go straight on to reach a T-junction of tracks at the hill top. Keep straight on; the path levels off, then drops down through a dense conifer plantation to cross another track.

C The edge of the forest is reached at a gate; ahead can be seen the ruined buildings of Teignhead Farm, occupied from 1808–1943. Once through the gate, turn left to enter Teignhead

Within Fernworthy Forest

The **Grey Wethers** stone circles are the source of various tales. Legend has it that on account of their resembling a flock of sheep – from a distance! – they were sold as such to a newcomer by a canny local; the deal was struck in the Warren House Inn. Another story relates how local unfaithful wives were forced to kneel in front of one of the stones; true repentance (or innocence) was rewarded by the stone remaining upright; guilt was proved by the stone falling on the unfortunate woman and crushing her to death.

Newtake and follow the rough path across the open moor, which runs about 30ft (10m) from the wall bordering the forest. Cross a broken-down granite wall; at this point the forest wall bears away left; keep straight on (parts of this path can be boggy). Look ahead to pick out a drystone wall which runs from Sittaford Tor 1,765 ft (538m) on the right along the skyline to reach the forest wall on the left. Pass through a gate in the wall and go straight ahead to reach Grey Wethers stone circles. These were partially restored around the turn of the century, by which time only about one third of the stones were still standing. In late Victorian times some people felt that the stones had been dressed – they are unusually rectangular – but they are all natural.

? *What is the name of the granite bridge crossed at the start of point* **B** *?*

D Retrace your steps to the drystone wall, and turn right. At the forest edge turn right, and pick your way across tussocky moorland along the wall; the land drops steeply down to meet a spring in a small valley (boggy at times). Where the spring passes under the forest wall, turn left over an unmarked ladder-stile to re-enter the forest.

E Walk straight on along a gritty track, which soon meets another on a bend; turn right downhill. The track then leads slightly uphill; ignore the track coming in sharp right, and keep straight on to meet another gritty track on a bend, with a grassy track coming in from the right. Turn left; the track runs downhill to cross the stream, then bends right to follow the stream back to the granite bridge crossed at the start of point **B**.

F Turn right on the lane to cross the bridge, then left on a track to leave the lane and pass through the gate by the bird hide. Retrace your steps back to the end of the woods; do not turn right up the track but keep straight on along the edge of the reservoir to have a better look at the dam. At times of low water hut circles are visible at the edge of the reservoir here. Turn right to walk through the picnic area and back to the car park. ●

Ponies at Grey Wethers

Harford and the Erme Valley

This walk explores a very quiet and unexpectedly lovely corner of Dartmoor. You are unlikely to stumble across the pretty little hamlet of Harford and the delightful valley of the Erme en route to anywhere else; and, once discovered, it is a secret you will probably want to keep to yourself.

START Harford

DISTANCE 5 miles (8km)

TIME 2½ hours

PARKING By the church in Harford, signposted from Ivybridge

ROUTE FEATURES Riverside path wet and rocky in places; steep ascent up lane from railway viaduct to Pithill Farm

19

Park by the church, on the lane leading to Harford Gate. Notice the little well in the wall opposite the lychgate. Walk back to Harford Cross and turn right, passing the church on the right. Follow the quiet lane downhill to cross Harford Bridge; there was a bridge here in the 16th century, and it is possible that part of the existing structure dates from the original. Follow the lane uphill under huge beech trees to reach the entrance to Hall Farm on the right.

Ⓐ Turn left through a wooden gate, following footpath signs for Ivybridge, and down the granite-walled green lane, with almost parkland-like-farmland to left and right. The swell of Butterdon Hill can be seen ahead and to the left. The track ends at a boggy area; pick your way across and through a gate into a field, with a granite wall on the left. Where the wall veers left keep straight on uphill, aiming for a gap in the wooded bank ahead. At the gap, a path sign directs you straight ahead, keeping the coniferous plantation on the left.

PUBLIC TRANSPORT None available

REFRESHMENTS None en route; picnic tables by the Erme river during point Ⓒ; Cornwood Inn and tearoom 2½ miles (4km) from Harford

PUBLIC TOILETS None en route

ORDNANCE SURVEY MAPS Explorer OL28 (Dartmoor), Landranger 202 (Torbay & South Dartmoor)

What will happen to you if you try to cross Harford Bridge in a vehicle that is more than 7ft (2.1m) wide?

B A path sign directs you left through a gate; this runs downhill through woodland to pass through two gates and into an old oak wood, with wonderful old granite walls, grassy glades and rowan trees. Leave this wood via a small wooden gate in a granite wall.

C Turn left, signed 'Ivybridge via Erme valley'. This narrow wooded path leads steeply downhill to meet the River Erme, where you turn right to follow the river downstream. The source of the Erme lies seven miles (11.3km) north of Harford, in one of the remotest parts of the southern moor, near the sources of the Avon and Plym. The first part of the route along the river is unkempt and a little uneven; it passes over a railed wooden footbridge before tackling a couple of old granite walls and negotiating a boggy patch, but it is all quite passable. The next footpath sign directs you away from the river, then over a ladder-stile into a coniferous plantation. The path becomes easier, and the river speeds up to tumble through a series of narrow gorges, with waterfalls and deep pools in

By Harford Bridge

next path sign directs you ahead through a metal gate and along a gritty track between high banks. At the top of the track there are two metal gates ahead; go through the gate on the right. A path sign directs you straight ahead along the track, with wonderful views of Butterdon Hill 1,204ft (367m) and Western Beacon 1,089ft (332m) – stone quarried from here was used to build the viaduct – to the right. The track leads to a metal gate; pass through that, then through a wooden gate and cattle-grid at the remote house at Wilkey's Moor, which is passed on the right. Pass to the right of the barn, and ahead through a wooden gate to enter a lovely area of granite walls

deciduous woodland, complete with picnic tables. Follow the broad track on to pass a weir, then under the main Exeter–Penzance railway line viaduct to meet the road. The piers of the original viaduct (which had a wooden superstructure), built by Isambard Kingdom Brunel for the Great Western Railway, can be seen.

D Turn right up the road to pass under the viaduct again. Ignore the lane left; where the road bends sharp left, keep straight ahead on the tarmac lane, signed 'public footpath Hall Farm'. The lane ascends steeply through woodland, but is very quiet. Where two footpaths lead off right into the valley, and another leads off left, keep on the lane, which leaves the woodland and levels off to end at a T-junction with Pithill Cottage and farm on the right. Turn left; the

The **Two Moors Way** runs across Butterdon Hill, which can be seen over the Erme valley during the walk. This 102-mile (163km) long-distance footpath runs from Ivybridge to Lynmouth on the north coast of Devon, linking the Dartmoor and Exmoor National Parks. It provides a wonderfully varied walking route, and joins up with a number of other trails, for example the South West Coast Path, the Tarka Trail, and the Dartmoor Way. It was opened on May 29, 1976.

Looking towards Butterdon Hill

and oak trees. Walk across the next field, through a gap in the bank, and straight across the next field, aiming for a wooden gate in the bank (the outward route drops down to the River Erme at this point).

E Retrace your steps through the woodland, up through the coniferous plantation, and right across the fields to rejoin the walled track to Hall Farm. Once on the lane turn right and follow the lane back over Harford Bridge to your car. Have a good look at St Petrock's Church. There is evidence of a church here around the Norman Conquest, and definitely by 1262; the present building dates to the late 15th early 16th centuries, and has a painted memorial to John Prideaux, a local man who became the Bishop of Worcester. The old granite cross by the lychgate was moved here in 1909, and was a waymarking cross, originally on the old route from Plympton to South Brent; the lane to the moor was known as 'the Brent road' in the 18th century.

> The upper reaches of the **Erme** hold one of the densest concentrations of **Bronze Age remains** on Dartmoor, including the longest stone row (possibly the longest in the world) which runs north–south for 2¼ miles (3.6km) and crosses the Erme and the Redlake. It was also a rich tin-mining area in medieval times; a good example of a tinner's hut can be seen on the west bank of the river about three miles (4.8km) north of Harford. These domed 'beehive' huts were made of granite, and used for storing tools and equipment.

Meldon Reservoir and Blackator Copse

20

START Meldon Reservoir

DISTANCE 5 miles (8km)

TIME 2½ hours

PARKING Car park (contributions cairn) at Meldon Reservoir, signposted from Okehampton

ROUTE FEATURES Rough approach over moor to Black Tor; rocky path through Blackator Copse

This is a walk for those who want to experience all that the high moor has to offer – but without going too far off the beaten track! The route passes within striking distance of Dartmoor's highest tors, and returns via a magical ancient woodland and remote river valley, giving the impression that you really are miles from anywhere: yet the whole package lies within minutes of the A30.

Leave the car park via the steps next to the toilets, through the kissing-gate and turn left, signed 'bridleway to the moor'. The tarmac way drops down to cross the reservoir dam via a metal gate. Look left here to see Meldon viaduct, now a scheduled ancient monument, built in 1874 when the London and South Western Railway line was extended to Lydford. It towers 150ft (45.75m) above the valley of the West Okement River, and is 541ft (165m) across. The dam was built between 1970-72 at a cost of £1.6 million, and is huge: 660ft (201m) long and 145ft (44.25m) high – an amazing 191 steps lead down into the valley of the West Okement below. The reservoir acts as a top-up supply for nearby Prewley Treatment Works.

Two hundred years ago, the **Meldon** area was exploited for tin, copper, limestone, roadstone and aplite, arsenic, copper, granite and chert. Formerly owned by British Rail, the quarry covers an area of 235 acres (95ha), and produces ballast, roadstone, concrete aggregates and building stone. During the 19th century there was a copper mine near here on Black Down.

PUBLIC TRANSPORT None available

REFRESHMENTS None en route; range of pubs and cafés in Okehampton; picnic area by the reservoir

PUBLIC TOILETS In car park

ORDNANCE SURVEY MAPS Explorer OL28 (Dartmoor), Landranger 191 (Okehampton & North Dartmoor)

A Once over the dam, turn right and follow the broad, gritty track along the edge of the reservoir. Where a stile over the fence on the right leads to a waterside picnic area, follow the track as it veers left and up the long, gradual ascent of Longstone Hill, with excellent views of the quarry and viaduct. You can still hear the A30 here, but as the track veers right around the end of the hill the only evident sign of civilisation is the line of red-and-white posts along Black Down, marking the edge of the military ranges. It is possible to walk within the ranges except on live firing days, providing you don't touch any military debris.

B Just beyond the valley of the Red-a-ven Brook on the left the track (now vague and grassy) splits; keep to the left fork; at the next fork keep right. Dartmoor's highest points can be seen above left: Yes Tor 2,031ft (619m) and, just over the skyline, High Willhays 2,037ft (621m). The path becomes less distinct as Black Tor is approached; aim for the right-hand outcrop.

C On reaching Black Tor, turn left to walk past the second outcrop, which rises to 1,601ft (488m). From here you can get excellent views up the West Okement valley into the remote heartland of Dartmoor.

Blackator Copse, owned by the Duchy of Cornwall, is one of the best areas of ancient high altitude oak woodland in Britain and is established as a National Nature Reserve. **Wistman's Wood**, (see Walk 16) **Piles Copse** and **Blackator Copse** all share the same magical atmosphere.

? *In what year did Blackator Copse become a National Nature Reserve?*

Retrace your steps to the first outcrop, drop over the edge of the hill and pick your way down into the valley. Blackator Copse covers the slopes below Black Tor. To get a proper feel of this enchanting place, turn left at the river to enter the woodland. It is well worth walking to the far end; *the path is very rocky at times, and boggy at others,* but the experience should not be missed – and the banks of the West Okement provide an ideal picnic spot.

D Retrace your steps back to the lower end of the copse. Note how barren the opposite bank is: the broad swell of Corn Ridge, rising to 1,762ft (537m), sweeps up and away from the river, devoid of vegetation and covered with clitter, caused by the erosive forces of freeze–thaw on granite boulders. Follow the river downstream; the path is indistinct and occasionally boggy. Where a small enclosure around the river is reached, keep close to the right wall; the land here is pretty wet. Just beyond the enclosure the path becomes more obvious, and passes a waterfall and a weir. The river runs through a deep valley, with pretty oak and rowan trees, to emerge at a level, marshy area known as Vellake Corner. Follow the path along the bottom of the slope on the right, passing a wooden footbridge on the left. *(An alternative return route starts here: cross the footbridge, then the stone bridge over the river; climb over a stile, turn right up steps, and follow the path to the right, to a gate. The path runs above the reservoir, ending at a gate; cross the path to a second gate, then left and right into the car park.)*

E Follow the narrow, gritty path on along the edge of the reservoir; the path runs right to cross a small stream on a wooden railed footbridge, then back towards the reservoir to rejoin the main track where it starts to curve up Longstone Hill. Keep left, and retrace your steps back to the dam and your car. ●

Further Information

Walking Safety

Although the reasonably gentle countryside that is the subject of this book offers no real dangers to walkers at any time of the year, it is still advisable to take sensible precautions and follow certain well-tried guidelines.

Always take with you both warm and waterproof clothing and sufficient food and drink. Wear suitable footwear such as strong walking boots or shoes that give a good grip over stony ground, on slippery slopes and in muddy conditions. Try to obtain a local weather forecast and bear it in mind before you start. Do not be afraid to abandon your proposed route and return to your starting point in the event of a sudden and unexpected deterioration in the weather.

All the walks described in this book will be safe to do, given due care and respect, even during the winter. Indeed, a crisp, fine winter day often provides perfect walking conditions, with firm ground underfoot and a clarity unique to this time of the year.

The most difficult hazard likely to be encountered is mud, especially

The Pepper Pot, Chagford

Jay's Grave

when walking along woodland and field paths, farm tracks and bridleways – the latter in particular can often get churned up by cyclists and horses. In summer, an additional difficulty may be narrow and overgrown paths, particularly along the edges of cultivated fields. Neither should constitute a major problem provided that the appropriate footwear is worn.

Follow the Country Code
- Enjoy the countryside and respect its life and work
- Guard against all risk of fire
- Take your litter home
- Fasten all gates
- Help to keep all water clean
- Keep your dogs under control
- Protect wildlife, plants and trees
- Keep to public paths across farmland
- Take special care on country roads
- Leave livestock, crops and machinery alone
- Make no unnecessary noise
- Use gates and stiles to cross fences, hedges and walls
                 (The Countryside Agency)

Useful organisations
Campaign to Protect Rural England
CPRE National Office, 128 Southwark Street, London SE1 0SW
Tel. 020 7981 2800
www.cpre.org.uk

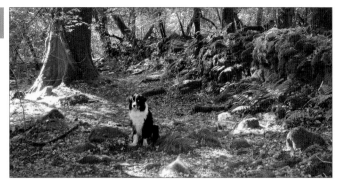

In the Erme Valley woodlands

Countryside Agency
John Dower House, Crescent Place, Cheltenham GL50 3RA
Tel. 01242 521381
www.countryside.gov.uk

English Heritage
23 Savile Row, London W1S 2ET
Tel. 020 7973 3212
www.english-heritage.org.uk

English Nature
Northminster House, Peterborough, Cambridgeshire PE1 1UA
Tel. 01733 455101
www.english-nature.org.uk

National Trust
Membership and general enquiries
PO Box 39, Warrington WA5 7WD
Tel. 0870 458 4000
www.nationaltrust.org.uk
Devon Office:
Killerton House, Broadclyst,
Exeter EX5 3LE
Tel. 01392 881691

Ordnance Survey
Romsey Road, Maybush, Southampton SO16 4GU
Tel. 08456 05 05 05 (Lo-call)

Public Transport:
For all public transport enquiries in south west England:
Tel. 0870 6082608

Ramblers' Association
2nd Floor, Camelford House, 87-90 Albert Embankment, London SE1 7TW
Tel. 020 7339 8500
www.ramblers.org.uk

Royal Society for the Protection of Birds (RSPB)
The Lodge, Sandy, Beds SG19 2DL

Tel. 01767 680551
www.rspb.org.uk

West Country Tourist Board
60 St Davids Hill, Exeter EX4 4SY
Tel. 01392 276351
www.wctb.co.uk

Dartmoor National Park Authority
information centres (*not open all
year round):
*Haytor: 01364 661520
*Newbridge: 01364 631303
*Postbridge: 01822 880272
Princetown: 01822 890414

Other tourist information centres:
Bovey Tracey: 01626 832047
South Dartmoor (Ivybridge):
01752 897035

Okehampton: 01837 53020
Tavistock: 01822 612938
Totnes: 01803 863168

Youth Hostels Association
Trevelyan House, Dimple Road,
Matlock, Derbyshire DE4 3YH
Tel. 01629 592600
www.yha.org.uk

Ordnance Survey Maps
Explorers
OL28 (Dartmoor)
110 (Torquay & Dawlish),
112 (Launceston & Holsworthy)

Landrangers
191 (Okehampton & North
Dartmoor)
202 (Torbay & South Dartmoor)

Ponies at Blackator Copse

Answers to Questions

Walk 1: 1845.

Walk 2: They are rabbits or hares, a pre-Christian fertility symbol which links Chagford with ancient China.

Walk 3: Three.

Walk 4: At the house called 'Where the Woozle Wasn't' near Hayne Cross.

Walk 5: 1881 D. Radford (who was responsible for piping a spring and providing three taps, so improving the village water supply).

Walk 6: 1893.

Walk 7: By horse-drawn cart and steam lorry (information board near the shop/café entrance).

Walk 8: May 1929.

Walk 9: You are not allowed to swim; but you can go fly fishing (if you get a licence).

Walk 10: 20%.

Walk 11: From top to bottom: fox, deer, badger.

Walk 12: An otter; the name of the trail is attributed to North Devon author Henry Williamson's classic story *Tarka the Otter*.

Walk 13: They are corbels, cut in 1903 for work on London Bridge, but excess to requirements.

Walk 14: Alfred James Hill (1889–1972), choirman, ringer and churchwarden, and John Clayton (1891–1973), parish treasurer.

Walk 15: Carrington, a local poet, who was born in Plymouth.

Walk 16: Four.

Walk 17: April 28, 1879 at the age of 85 (to be found on a plaque by the west window in Leusdon church).

Walk 18: Sandeman Bridge.

Walk 19: You will get stuck.

Walk 20: 1996; the answer is given on a noticeboard at the lower edge of the copse.